MW00941058

GOLF STORIES FROM THE STARS TO THE STALLS

ADVENTURES, ENCOUNTERS AND EXPERIENCES FROM ALL AROUND THE WORLD

LUCIANO ROCCIA

Translated from Italian

Translator Ross Wilkins
(rosswilkins71@gmail.com)

Copyright © 2017 Luciano Roccia
All rights reserved.

INTRODUCTION

H ouston Texas 1963. I was studying at the Baylor University, preparing my graduate thesis with two pioneers of cardiac surgery: Denton Cooley and Michael Debakey. The governor of the Rotary Club of Turin, where my father was a member, had given me a letter of presentation to give to his colleague in Houston. When I introduced myself, I was immediately invited to a dinner with all the 'rotarians' in the city. It was here that I met his daughter who offered to be my guide in Houston and the surroundings for a few days. She accompanied me one Saturday to a Golf Club where there was a charity tournament sponsored by the Rotary club. It was my first encounter with a golf course.

MICHAEL (my first instructor)

One year later, and now graduated, I was doing my military service when I met Patricia, an English girl who had arrived to live in the neighborhood. We fell in love. Beautiful, tall, blonde with clear blue eyes she was a magnificent union of English and Egyptian.

Patricia's father, major Michael Bracey Gibbon was working for the intelligence services at the English Consulate in Turin. I invited him and his whole family to spend a Sunday in September at 'La Margherita', our family farm and my father's summer residence. It was 1964 and I became directly involved with golf for the first time.

Patricia's father had asked, before our meeting in the countryside, if there were any lawns and if it was worth bringing along his golf bag to practice a few shots. We had just collected the last bails of hay, the fields were perfectly flat with fresh green grass just beginning to regrow. After lunch we set off, Michael carrying his golf bag with me following.

When we arrived at the field he let a ball fall to the ground, took out an iron, and after a couple of warm up swings he hit the ball which landed at the foot of the tree at which he'd taken aim. He had old style clubs with wooden shafts and heads, he informed me, were forged by hand.

In the fields there were still some large hay bales that had been gathered the previous day. He took aim at one of these and with a perfect swing the ball landed on top. It all seemed so easy.

To my eyes Michael seemed like a great player. I didn't know that golf could present so many problems and challenges and that it was a famously difficult sport to master, so when asked if I wanted to try, I already played many other sports well, I accepted with enthusiasm, determined to show what I was made of.

The first swing and I clumsily broke the shaft of the club that he had just handed me. I hit the rock hard ground with maximum force. I looked down in shock at the club that I continued to hold while also slowly becoming aware of a strong pain in my elbow and the right side of my back. The impact of the strike on the ground had channeled along my arm as far as my neck. I was embarrassed but despite this he invited me to try again offering me another club. I did not accept the offer.

I followed him for a few hours carrying his bag, continually refusing his requests to try again, until we returned home. Michael congratulated my father and told him that the land would make a magnificent golf course.

My father gave him a strange look and smiled. He was probably thinking about the Dutch cows that he'd bought just a few days ago. They had just arrived from Holland and were already grazing in the fields.

From then on Michael would often come to 'play' at La Margherita, bringing with him red and white surveyors poles, bought at a hardware store, placing them, like flags, in various positions around the course as he played.

During this period I was so busy with my duties as a young surgeon, always on call at the emergency room, that I was only able to accompany him on rare occasions. I tried to learn something, at least not to break the shaft again, but I continued to use the club like a hoe, to shoot the air and on the few occasions that I actually hit the ball it went where it wanted and never where I wanted.

During the summer I joined him to play by the sea at the Arenzano Golf Club, it was a beautiful day and very hot.

I preferred to go down to the beach and bathe with Patrizia, refreshing ourselves and hiding in a small cave where the sea entered with a deafening rush wrapping us in foam. At the end of the summer Michael left Turin and I saw him only to say goodbye. He didn't want to take his old golf bag back to England and he asked me to keep it as a memento and implored me to continue playing golf, something that I had absolutely no intention of doing. Some of these clubs can be found today hanging in my club restaurant. Only many years later would I recall this episode and my first experience as a golf "hoer".

TEN YEARS LATER

I t was the 70s, Frank Warren, in addition to practicing as a psychiatrist in New York, was also the manager of some of the most famous doctors *in America*. I met him in San Francisco during a seminar on acupuncture which I was holding for the California Society of Anesthesiologists.

He asked if I had a manager and when he discovered that not only did I not have a manager but for this seminar I would receive only miserly expenses. He realized my naivety and informed me that in the US all conferences were paid. He immediately became the manager of my conferences and my courses for doctors in the U.S. taking 10% of my earnings and making me a whole lot of money.

In Madison, Wisconsin, during a congress, he asked if I played golf. I made the mistake of telling him that years before I had played but that I wasn't much good. There was nothing for it. I was obliged to follow him and other colleagues to the municipal golf course, in the centre of a magnificent public park, where as well as the golf course there were also tennis courts. I didn't want to play and make a fool of myself, but it was impossible to resist their urging.

The first shot, I didn't manage to hit the ball, I made an 'air shot' from which I narrowly escaped a dislocated shoulder. The second try I shanked, skimming the heads of my colleagues, almost making a hole in a car windscreen and landed at the foot of the net surrounding the tennis courts. The oblivious tennis players turned on hearing the crash of the ball against the car. My companions no longer insisted I play anymore and I became Frank's caddie.

A few years later during a sailing trip around Corsica, I landed with my sailboat at Portovecchio. I was moored alongside some English boats. Everyone had to remain in port for a few days due to the 'Mistral' wind which, with a force in excess of 40 knots, made any type of sailing dangerous. I made friends with my neighbors, mainly because the aroma of our cooking reached their boats, obliging me to invite them one evening for dinner. After two days of enforced inactivity, spent on long walks and inland excursions, one morning I saw my neighbors leave their boat with some golf bags and wait for a taxi. They immediately invited me to join their group and, accepting their kind offer, I left with them. This is how I discovered the Sperone Golf Club, a splendid golf course on the rocks of Corsica. One of the English guys insisted that I play and suggested that I use only an iron, in his opinion this would makes things much easier. With their sage advice I managed to play a few holes and enjoy myself although I did lose several balls in the sea. It had been a long time since I had held a club in my hand.

Following this experience I continued my involved with golf, but this time more from a financial point of view with an investment that came up trumps. A few years later Allegra Agnelli proposed that I buy shares in the Golf Club I Roveri (today the Royal Park), recently founded by her husband Umberto. I accepted, acquiring a certain number of shares that just a few years later I sold for five times my original investment, without having played golf once. While on this subject, I remember the time that I hosted the son in law of a Canadian colleague who came to Italy on honeymoon. He wanted to play golf and I invited him to 'I Roveri'. When he returned that evening, he described, emotionally, his day. He was a good player and he'd really enjoyed himself, he was captivated by the beautiful course and grounds and more, during the round he met another solitary golfer, who stayed with him, chatting until the end of the round. His accidental golf companion then invited him to lunch during which he discovered that he was the "Boss of Fiat". It was Umberto Agnelli. A great man who was a patient of mine for many years and of whom I have wonderful memories.

1985

R oberto Falda was a colleague of mine and a golfer. One day I told him about Michael and my golf experience. He arrived on a Sunday in autumn to meet us at La Margherita with a group of golfing friends armed with a couple of clubs. I took them around the course, where they enjoyed playing and practically followed the same route that Michael had played many years before. They also repeated what Michael had told my father many years before: "perfect land for a golf course". It was the autumn of 1985.

It was on this day that I started the project "Country Club La Margherita". With Roberto there was Beppe, an engineer and passionate golfer who had developed a course to be built in Chieri, a course never realized due to bureaucratic red tape. This had remained a 'thorn in his side' so when he saw my interest in the idea of a course he asked for a plan of the farm showing the positions of the irrigation sprinklers already present and asked if he could plan and design a theoretical course but without any obligation on my part. I accepted and supplied all the requested information. It was already the Spring of 1986.

This is how the project, Country Club La Margherita began, which would also include the Golf Club La Margherita, an 18 hole course which, due to the topography of the land, would, according to the experts, be one of the most beautiful in Piedmont. Alongside the already existing buildings: the riding centre with adjoining covered riding school, the well equipped veterinary hospital, the Piedmont Club of ultra light flying, 2 pools and a farm with guest quarters and restaurant.

When I talked about the idea with friends and patients, almost everyone thought I was mad, saying that nobody would come to play golf in Carmagnola, a sport that was only for the rich who play in magnificent parks like La Mandria, the noble and ancient hunting ground transformed into a public park and residential village for the high society of Turin. They were so wrong! Just like many years before, my medical colleagues had been wrong when I decided to study acupuncture, they called me a witch doctor, or when the local farmers thought I was mad when I contracted the first Biogas installation converting animal dung into methane to heat my home.

A few weeks later Beppe and Roberto returned to La Margherita, with a beautiful colored design illustrating the position of the future 18 hole course at the "La Margherita Golf Club". The engineer had brought along a surveyor who carried a bag containing, 18 red and white poles for measuring, just like those I saw Michael use many years before. The difference this time was that following the project design for the first time the exact distance from the start of each future hole to the position of the flag was measured. And Beppe and Roberto immediately started to test shots in order to study the course. They only used a few clubs, compared to those used normally and in a few hours practically the whole course was traced out.

When they'd finished they asked if they could leave the poles on the course as they wanted to bring a professional golfer friend to try the course. This is how I met, for the first time, Dino Canonica, one of the 'forgotten' craftsmen of project 'La Margherita'. He came a few days later with Beppe, Roberto and Angelo, another golf friend, again offering his advice, modifying the course and, based on his experience as an instructor, avoiding the risk of crossing-over and possible accidents between players.

So the first real project "Golf Club La Margherita" was born, taking its name from its parent farm. In order to realize the project we needed to promote it in order to find financing members for the construction. As well as a brochure explaining the proposed "Country Club La Margherita" we decided to organize a driving range on a field bordering the main road; visible to passing motorists. At the same time I began digging the foundations of a building, for which I already had planning permission, intended as a saddlery and company recreation club, which would later be modified to become the Club House.

On Sundays, Roberto and his friends came to practice on the driving range and later played on the fields of the future course. In any case, word of a new golf club had spread around the golf world and, not infrequently, golfers or aspiring golfers, came to see. At the hospital I often talked about the project with colleagues about my intention to develop a natural biological golf course. We had also found a young instructor who came at weekends to give lessons.

Beppe should have created a company to continue the project but it was all taking too long and despite numerous requests, from many golfers to become founding members, the company and construction never took off. Myself, completely ignorant of golf affairs left the 'experts' in charge of the project until I tired of the delays and dissolved the group. I organised the financing of the project myself, I invited about 50 friends and colleagues for drinks at my home, during which I presented the designs and a programme for the construction of the club to be realized in a few weeks. Within a few hours I had about ten people signed up and the funds that permitted me to begin work. The first to sign on was obviously my friend Marzio Panichi and close behind him, my colleagues at the hospital. We built a very basic four hole course and adapted some farmhouses as the headquarters of the club, here began our first problems. Word had spread about the new initiative and on Sundays players arrived who fell in love with the place and wanted to become members of the club.

At the same time they gave suggestions for improvements to the course and possible future developments. I didn't know who to turn to. Piero Cora, my childhood friend and great golfer, came to mind. He was an adviser to the Italian Golf Federation and vice president of the most prestigious golf course in Turin. Together we founded the Golf Club La Margherita and Piero took the situation in hand managing the construction and developing one of the most beautiful golf courses in Italy. It was 1987. It was immediately clear that the rapidly constructed four holes would not satisfy the ambitions of the hardened golfers aspiring to become members of the new club, not least because the unspoilt countryside of the area, with a spectacular view of the Alps and Monviso, meant the new course was located in an enviably beautiful setting. The new Board took the initial project in hand, modifying it and developing it into a classic American course, with fields that had little to do with the typical Piedmont countryside, and with projects for additions to the course, a pool, a clubhouse and so on, worthy of a luxury course. Some of these projects conflicted with my rustic and natural spirit, but I absolutely couldn't interfere, lacking as I was in any experience in the organization of a golf club, even if I did have experience of developing a sailing club, a horse riding club, a flying club and many other enterprises in other non sporting areas. As the owner of the land and founder of the course I was part of the Board, I was shocked to discover several quotes for work which were accepted only because they were presented by companies who worked exclusively in the golfing world, and were part of a certain environment (and were considered a cartel) . Many of these quotes were not at all competitive with those of other good companies unknown, however, in golfing circles.

Ultimately, costs skyrocketed and transformed into an outlay that was anything but economical, good cost management flew out of the window. The membership fees imposed were rather high and I was constantly shocked that none of the members protested when presented with checks that I, in my naivety as a new entrepreneur, considered excessive even if shared by all the members. For example: if a certain quote was higher than another, a single businessman would certainly have considered this unacceptable and looked at other possibilities. If, however, this additional amount is to be divided between 200 investors, the impact is considered irrelevant. When I put myself in the position of a member and complained about this waste of money the response was always; "do you expect a golf member to question 50,000 lire more (50 $) for the level of service offered by our club"?

All contracts were assigned following a rule of preference for those firms considered "golf suppliers". Without this qualification they would not even be considered. I remember a classic example of a micro granular fertilizer, sold in 1 kg sacks labeled "accredited for golf courses" cost the equivalent of 1.50 euros today. Years later I discovered that the same product in 10kg sacks used in agriculture, fruit and vegetable production, cost just 30 euro cents a kilo. This was the way for almost everything supplied to a golf course. In the following years, I wrote a number of articles, which attracted a lot of criticism, on what I call the "golf mafia". These companies took advantage of the fact that golf was played almost exclusively by well off people who didn't pay attention to costs and therefore could easily be 'taken advantage of,' as I often said to my friend Carlo Bordogna. In many articles about golf, golfers were portrayed by many journalists as rich and stupid, my experience at this time confirms this assertion. Now things have changed. Golf has become more widespread; businessmen have entered into its world who manage clubs like companies, scrutinizing the finances, to close the year without requesting extra payments from members to cover losses due to excessive spending. During this change in the golf world 'Golfimpresa' was born, a consortium of private golf clubs who supply structures and services to various amateur sport associations. The golf mafia however, if not to the same extent as the past, still exists.

Another episode that earned me the wrath of golf professionals was when, in a series of articles in 'Mondo del Golf –' Golf World magazine', they talked about golf as an expensive sport and not assessable to everyone. My response was published in which I asked why a ski instructor who taught in the cold, sometimes in the middle of a storm, risking a broken leg or worse, with all the responsibility for their students, often undisciplined and difficult children, earns just 15,000 lire an hour while a golf instructor earns 20,000 for just half an hour. Despite the fact that the latter usually works in beautiful surroundings, without risks to his health and with students of a certain age, who don't usually create problems. Nobody replied to my letter.

The employees of many golf clubs wouldn't want to talk to me anymore if I were to discuss their positions. There are many (and I stress not all) who just because they work in golf, after a course of just a few months, can make a wage the envy of many graduates and, above all, the envy of many of their colleagues with similar duties who I know in many clubs across Europe and America.

I abandoned the Management Committee and made a decision provoked by my son's friends who, when they came to meet us at La Margherita showed an interest in golf but at the same time said that they found is out of reach due to the high prices charged in Italy.

I remembered how Michael had enjoyed himself playing on natural fields many years before saying that he felt like he was on one of the many English golf courses that he'd played. He made a comparison between the very expensive Italian courses and English courses where you could play for the equivalent of a few dollars. He told me about an area near Birmingham, a mining area, where they had built a golf course and where the miners went to play and breathe the fresh air of the countryside, after many hours spent underground. I also remembered the golf courses in the US that I'd visited with Frank Warren that weren't 'manicured' in any way (an expression learnt from many Northern European golfers) and for this reason a round of golf only cost a few dollars.

I decided to construct a low cost golf course that would be managed at minimum cost and would therefore allow youngsters, like the friends of my son, to take up golf and so create a "Golf for All". This would become the motto of my Golf Club, very much criticized by other golfers at the time. At the same time reading an article in a Golf Magazine about diseases caused by chemical products used on many courses, I decided to create a fully 'biological', natural golf course without the use of weedkillers or other chemicals.

When La Margherita was opened I decided to start playing, a decision I would regret during the fifth lesson when my instructor, having complimented me on my swing, had the terrible idea of informing me that I had a gift for golf and that if I continued in this way, in about six months, I would be ready to play on the course. I had a vision of myself hitting balls on the driving range for six months hour after hour and I understood why so many of my friends had taken up golf only to give it up a short time later. Many had confessed to me that they found it a boring sport but I'd never understood why. A professional helped me to understand why.

I hung up the very expensive golf bag that I'd bought, rather frivolously, following advice from my instructor and for four years I didn't touch a golf club again. I concentrated on developing the course and the club, that in a couple of years had gained about two hundred members most of them friends of Piero or colleagues from the hospital.

Leaving the management committee, I decided to go on with the project of creating a new 'biological' golf course.

PETER

During my frequent trips abroad I visited many golf courses to get ideas, just as the Japanese had always done, copying everything that was worth copying, cars, above all, to become one of the richest economic and industrial forces in the world. I photographed splendid greens and any particularly interesting construction. It was on such a trip on the island of Santa Lucia where I was on holiday, at the home of my friend Enrico, that I happened upon a small golf course. It was a drizzly day at the beginning of the rainy season and the course was practically deserted, abandoned by the seasonal tourists.

In the tiny shack serving as an office-proshop, as well as a very bored employee, there was a helpful young man who presented himself as the club professional and immediately asked if I would like a golf lesson. Behind him on the wall was a board with, "one hour lesson (60 minutes) 10 dollars", written on it. A far cry from the Italian standard rate. I hadn't had any intention of taking a lesson but I was interested to see the course and considering the price, I found myself almost automatically accepting the invitation. I followed Peter, the instructor, to a green where I received my first real golf lesson and I'll explain now why I say real.

The five golf lessons I had taken four years previously, when I'd decided to give up, had at least left me with the memory of the base movement of the swing and after a short time, following the instructions of the my teacher, I began to hit the ball with a certain regularity. At this point Peter said, "come, let's go and play on the course".

On seeing my surprise he explained that as soon as his students hit the ball with regularity he preferred to continue lessons on the course, with him also playing. Even if students made errors, he explained, they learned to understand the rules and the difficulties of golf, difficulties that happen and can only be resolved by actually playing golf. On the driving range, he told me, you perfect your movement making it automatic but on the course you learn to play. I continued to closely study the instructor's swing and tried to imitate it. In this way students learn the game much faster and following instructions they actually enjoy themselves, becoming passionate about golf without risking dropping out of the game like many beginners who are obliged by their instructors to spend hours, weeks and months on the driving range. He was really right! We put a bag in the car and off we went.

The course was covered in a thick carpet of lush grass (dog's tooth grass) where each shot was helped significantly by the position of the ball on the grass, which seemed to be suspended above the ground, I found it rather easy to hit the ball, often managing to hit it in the desired direction: towards the flag and the hole. When by some miracle, beginners luck perhaps, at the second hole, the ball went in on the first putt and I heard the sound of the ball against the plastic of the cup, Golf, with a capital 'G', entered my blood. There were few people on the course, Peter was free and at the end of the first hour I told him I'd like to continue the lesson.

Despite my inexperience we managed to cover all 9 holes in little over two hours. I don't remember how many times I hit the ball, how many bad hits, how many went in the right direction, how many divots of grass I lifted or how many times I missed the ball completely, however, I do remember very well the enthusiasm when I holed a shot at the umpteenth putt. At the last hole Peter shook my hand. I felt like a real golfer.

We returned to the shack where we drank a beer and Peter explained to me that as the season was finishing and there weren't many tourists left he would be returning to work as a builder for a few months. He had a wife and kids. He had tried to become an instructor in the USA, but there was a large increase in the number of professionals and he had returned home where his building work allowed him to wait for the next tourist season. He earned three hundred dollars a month. I offered him five hundred, board and lodging with the return trip paid; he accepted and returned with me to La Margherita. He became the first golf instructor at the Girasoli.

CHRIS AND THE FLOATING DRIVING RANGE

In the small office of the golf club a golfer arrived, while I was chatting with Peter, who had been following us on the course. He was a likeable American who introduced himself, and when he realized that I was Italian and called Luciano, he gave me a nickname (something that happened to me a lot in the USA) – the name of the famous gangster " Lucky Luciano". He invited me for a drink on his boat, anchored at the marina in Marigot Bay. Chris had a splendid motorsailer, over 30 meters long with a skipper and crew. We sat down for a drink on a comfy sofa, served by a beautiful young girl.

When he realized that, as well as being a surgeon, I also practiced acupuncture he told me about his tennis elbow which bothered him a lot especially when he played golf. I told him that something could be done and I offered my services for treatment during my stay on the island. I asked in turn what he did and was informed that he was one of the most important estate agents in New York and that he spent the cold winter months sailing around the Caribbean. I was interested in knowing how he could manage his work in the middle of the sea and so far from the office. He invited me to go below deck, where I found myself in a large room furnished as an office with a number of employees working at computers. At his command, a large screen was switched on and after a few moments his partner in the New York office appeared, showing me that it was just like being in the office but via satellite, and that he could follow the everyday activities of his company from on board, even when sailing.

That same evening I returned to treat his elbow and given that the next day I would be leaving for the island of Grenadine, he invited me to accompany him so that I could continue his treatment. This was how I ended up spending five days sailing in the Caribbean administering acupuncture, not only to the skipper, but also other guests on board. Every evening we anchored in one or other splendid bay, Chris sent one of the crew members to place some floating poles with a flag at varying distances from the boat and we practiced our driving on a hundred or so balls. Before leaving the US they had loaded a thousand floating golf balls and after each training session a sailor would go out and collect them together with the poles. I met Chris a several times after, during my visits to New York. His 'tennis elbow' and his golf had improved.

I finally started to play golf. With Peter we opened the first driving range at the Girasoli. It was an immediate success, word carried around friends and my sons' friends and soon Peter was busy with lessons, not just in golf but also English. He was a handsome boy and word spread quickly through the female population; I can't really blame Peter for all the comings and goings at his lodgings. It seemed that Peter had a serious problem turning down any girl with white skin, even if they weren't particularly attractive.

During the construction of La Margherita I got to know Piero Bruno, surveyor and renowned constructor of golf courses, as well as an excellent player, as all golf course architects should be. I only knew architects that knew very little about golf. With Bruno we designed the first nine holes of Girasoli. Marcella, a member of La Margherita with whom we had discussions at the beginning of May, chose the name. " Your fields are full of flowers," she told me, " why not call it the Girasoli as these are the flowers that stand out the most"? Girasole is the name given in Piedmont to dandelion flowers. Due to its therapeutic diuretic property it is known in French as "pis en lit" or "piscialletto" – wet the bed. The members of the new Golf Club would become the harvesters of this plant which, due to the complete absence of any weedkiller on the course would be collected at the end of every day and prepared with boiled eggs and garlic cloves to make a delicious salad, typical of Piedmont cuisine. Girasoli was the first truly ecological and natural course in Italy. Ecological and natural in two ways: first for professional and ethical beliefs, and second, for economic reasons. Dedicated myself, in addition to surgery, to a holistic and natural medicine such as acupuncture, I absolutely had to make an ecological choice. Additionally, as I had started the project without help from anyone and was financing the whole project out of my own pocket, I had to make some serious economic choices. Most Italian golf courses are designed by architects who are more or less famous (usually English or American). Their signature gives kudos to the course. Certain projects cost almost as much, if not more, than the actual cost of the construction of the course. This happened at the majority of Italian courses constructed until a few years ago. I remember visiting a golf club, close to Rome, founded by a famous stylist. I was kindly accompanied by a member for a tour of the whole complex. At the end of the tour he confided in me that the maintenance costs of the clubhouse where higher, by a long way, than those of the course. In the USA, the most developed golf country, where the most famous golfers of all time were born and raised, the majority of normal courses, where 95% of American golfers play, are designed by ordinary players, in some cases professionals, leaving the natural terrain as it is, without modifications. Clubhouses, in the main, are almost non existent and, at best, other than a small reception and a drinks dispenser there is just a bathroom, without changing rooms, showers or the like. It's the course that counts. You arrive in the car park, you put your shoes on in the car, you play, you drink and eat perhaps a sandwich or a hamburger and go home to take a shower. This is the reason for the low cost of golf in many countries in particular in Anglo-Saxon nations. On the many courses that I've played, I've never seen anything quite as distasteful as green hills shaped into a pyramid, designed and realized, like a personal work of art, by a famous American architect at a private luxury course. The 'Girasoli' golf course, entirely respecting golfing tradition, was constructed on the same fields where hay was collected and where horses and cows grazed, enriching the natural vegetation in order to thicken the grassy mantle, though without selecting only one 'pure' type of grass. Only the greens are similar to the greens of other courses and in this area most of the infesting weeds are removed by hand or by applying much reduced quantities of herbicide selected for its low or lack of toxicity. For this reason 'selective' herbicides are not used on the fairways which represent 99% of the area of the golf course, unlike the majority of other courses where the grassy mantle is comprised of tropical grass and not native grass. This grass forms a perfect cover that, when cut, becomes smooth like a billiard table, but must be defended from infesting grasses that, with their different growth rates, render the surface uneven and not as perfect as the "spoiled" golfers would prefer. The products used to defend the grass, even if they spare the selected grass, in any case stress it making it susceptible to diseases that require the use of additional chemical pollutants. Among other things the use of these grasses, during the hot summer months requires large quantities of water, they need to be watered daily, instead, with native grasses weekly watering is more than enough. This is the reason that Green and ecological groups are often opposed to the construction of new courses. I have illustrated the problem a number of times in my many articles in the publication " Mondo del Golf" but above all noted in the most renowned American golf publication, "Golf Digest", in which the various diseases found in those who have been in contact with these substances have been listed. One of my colleagues, a dermatologist, told me that he recognized golfers by the lesions that many have on their legs.

As opposed to the majority of courses were the landscape is completely changed to follow the architect's project, practically no earth was moved to construct our course. This type of work, which also involves costly machinery, was limited to small areas essential for the construction of the greens and starting tees. The course was constructed following the natural contours of the softly, sloping land; nature was our architect.

The same irrigation system quoted at around 170 million Italian lira by a company specializing in the construction of golf courses, was constructed by myself and my agricultural employees, buying all the materials from agricultural suppliers at a total cost of just 35 million lira.

All these choices meant that the costs of construction were reduced to the absolute minimum and we built nine holes for the equivalent cost of 1 or 2 holes on a 'normal' course. Reduced construction costs also meant reduced maintenance charges which meant that the course was truly accessible to all. I still remember when professor Chimenti, President of the Federation, came to play on my course and asked how much I'd spent on the construction. When I told him he just didn't believe me.

THE SAHEL

P eter was my first real instructor and with him I started my first steps on the fairways of la Girasoli and other courses in Piedmont. I had been playing for almost a year when my work as a surgeon, for reasons too long to discuss and in spite of my no longer tender years, brought me into contact with an ONG (Non Government Organization) involved in Sanitary Cooperation in Africa on behalf of the Foreign Ministry. This was how I found myself working for the Red Crescent (Arabian Red Cross) in Mauritiana, during the war between Senegal and Mauritania over a stretch of jungle between the two countries. It was the end of September 1992. Mauritania was without doubt, one of the poorest countries of central Africa, in the Sahel desert, governed by a fundamental Marxist-Leninist regime. The capital, Nouakchott, was surrounded by a shantytown where, in their thousands, refugees from the area of the war collected without any medical assistance. It was my job to establish an emergency room in this city of refugees and re-establish, following years of closure and inactivity, a hospital in the region of Nema close to the border with Mali, an area populated by the Tuareg people and where there was a local, tribal war. I shuttled between Nema and Nouakchott traveling 18 hours on a ruined road in the middle of the desert. It was on this path that my local driver/interpreter, died one night, hitting a camel which unexpectedly crossed in front of him smashing the windscreen and killing him instantly, while I was sleeping on the back seat. I had to wait till dawn before a ramshackle vehicle with some passengers reached me. The passengers helped me to free the jeep from the dead camel and to bury my driver; in a hole dug out at the foot of a small hill a little way from the path. Fortunately the impact hadn't damaged the jeep's motor and even without a windscreen I managed to reach the capital after many hours, where it fell to me to deliver the bad news to the family and make a statement to the local authorities. The informed me that this type of accident was very common and wouldn't cause me any problems. During the first month of my stay, in addition to contracting malaria which was magically cured with herbs from a Chinese doctor, I often ate with the Bedouin and as I wasn't immunized against the local intestinal parasites I lost almost 22 pounds. Now and then I returned to the capital, I frequented a restaurant used by the few Europeans who were visiting for work or resided in Mauritania. The majority were French who for historical reasons (Mauritania is an ex French colony) were still living there, in the desert, in a fort defended by a military garrison of the Foreign Legion. They continued to maintain commercial contacts with other African countries. There were also many Italian ENI-AGIP workers who worked at drilling stations in search of oil in the middle of the desert. The second time I was in this particular restaurant I noticed, on the table, a paper with the sonorous title of "The Nouakchott Gazette". There was news about the country and the war with Senegal, but the thing that really struck me, there was a short article deep in the paper headed, more or less, "The Mauritania Golf Open was won by Mr. Gerard Philippe of Air France". I was shocked, because after a month in Mauritiana, except for a few oases in the desert and a small green patch on the periphery of the capital, where they had constructed some wells and vegetable gardens for the city, I had not seen fields or forests or other areas that could possibly support the presence of a golf course. When I asked the waiter and other Europeans if they had heard of such a thing, nobody knew anything. Obviously I immediately went to the Air France agency where an employee showed me to the office of Mr. Gerard and I waited for him to arrive. I immediately noticed a golf bag in the corner and, finally on the arrival of the owner, I would be able to satisfy my curiosity; I was to be disappointed. When I asked where the course was, with an ironic smile he told me that I would never be able to find it and it was essential that I went with his group of golf friends so we arranged a meeting for the next day. I insisted on more information so that I'd be able to at least take a look at the course in the meantime, after all, following a month in Mauritania, I knew how to get about and felt confident that I would find the course. He told me, again sarcastically, to be patient and I would have a nice surprise. I was becoming more and more inquisitive and that evening returned to the foreigners' restaurant (the only one in this strict, Muslim country where you could drink wine and beer). I didn't learn any more, it appeared that no-one knew anything. The next day, at midday, I arrived with my Land Rover at the meeting point leaving Nouakchott and on the road which led to the Atlantic Ocean. I was met by a row of five off-road vehicles full of passengers and in the back I noticed there were numerous golf bags. It wasn't a joke after all – as I'd been starting to imagine. There really were golfers. It was low tide and when we arrived at the beach the sea was out transforming the beach into a long flat of pressed smooth sand which everyone called the motorway of the sea because it was crossed by many vehicles in order to move from north to south and vice versa. You should know that most of the Sahel desert is rather flat with low dunes, except towards the interior where there are many hills which lead to some mountain chains. Towards the ocean the desert wind meets the wind from the ocean and together they form high dunes of sand which fall in peaks to the sea, impeding the movement of vehicles from the beach towards the internal desert, except in a few sunken areas where during the rare rains of winter the torrential storm rains create real valleys. These valleys, covered in lush vegetation, are the only access from the beach to the desert. The only place where vehicles can stop in case of mechanical problems. The motorway of the sea was, for this reason, littered with abandoned vehicles: Trucks, cars, off-road vehicles, partly destroyed, which had had the misfortune to suffer a flat tire and that the high tide had blocked forever. Alongside these vehicles there were others: commercial fishing boats and small boats flung by the force of the sea onto the beach. I had already traveled this street a number of times, to reach a fishing village in Banc d'Arguin, a national park where I went to vaccinate children and where I had a unique experience: fishing with the inhabitants of the village with the help of dolphins and a very special technique. From the shore we entered the ocean to a distance of about 300 meters where the water was no deeper than 1.5 meters. On the beach, on a high wooden tower, an old fisherman, with acute eye sight, started to yell when he spotted a group of fish nearby. On this signal the fishermen, all in a row carrying a net hundreds of meters long on their shoulders, moved towards the high sea, the water reaching almost to their throats. The smaller fishermen jumped out of the water in order to breathe, and they separated to open the net and to form a large barrier. I too found myself behind this barrier with my video camera filming this scene next to another group of fishermen who on a second call from the old fisherman, started to pummel the sea with their hands, others with short branches or old pan lids. Unexpectedly I found myself assisting in this unforgettable spectacle. To the sides of us groups of dolphins appeared, as if at a signal they began to jump out of the sea creating an acrobatic show, moving towards the noise and swimming by my side, pushing the group of fish, spotted a little earlier, towards land and behind the unavoidable net awaiting them. I was very excited. My luck was my height that allowed me see over the group of fishermen and film the whole scene, with the fish, trapped jumping high, trying to clear the obstacle and the fishermen behind the net knocking them back with hands, branches and pan lids. The dolphins, swimming among us, caught a few fish that had escaped or that were purposely left as rewards for collaborating with the fishermen. At the same time the two ends of the net were pulled ahead, forming a circular trap which was slowly dragged to the shore where the women were already gathering to collect the fish which once dried in the sun would be sold be the villagers. I found out later, to my surprise that the village produced an excellent botargo that was bought by an Italian and exported to Sardegna. Along the marine road that led to the village I had often seen dolphins and other cetaceans beached and, unfortunately, dead, easy prey for the wolves and foxes of the desert that, when approached by man, ran away. Thus making way for the marvelous, enormous, white desert eagles happily feasting, tearing off, with their raptorial beaks, large pieces of meat. As opposed to other predators, when I approached with my video camera, the eagles didn't fly away, but continued with their meal indifferent and not disturbed in the least by my presence. Yes, I knew this street very well and I couldn't imagine where you would find a golf course. Suddenly the convey of cars turned into one of the rare valleys that were the only access to the desert. We traveled about 10-20 meters and the caravan came to a halt. Philippe came over while I observed the passengers from the various cars unload their golf bags. I looked around and saw only high sand dunes with many bushes in an environment of magnificent color where the only sound was that of the wind coming off the sea. As I got out of the car I saw one of the group descend with a bag full of flags and turning to Philippe he asked how many par fives he'd like today. At this moment he turned to me and explained, "this is our golf course and every time we change it according to how we'd like to play!" He introduced his companions, there were about twelve of them, representing almost all the diplomatic entities in Mauritania, from the French consulate to the German ambassador, American commercial entities and English cultural bodies and yet others that I can't recall, except the chief of police, a Frenchman who had invited me a number of times to dinner at his home (finally, an excellent Bordeaux instead of the imitation non-alcoholic wines). In the group there were two young ladies who, following a quick introduction left the group to lie on the beach and enjoy the sun. It was almost half an hour before the unfortunate player, whose turn it was to plant the flags, finished 'planting' the course under the relentless sun. The flags flapped on the dunes and green areas on the floor of the valley. When it was time for the tee shot I noted that every golf bag had a rubber squeegee, that piece of kit which you find yourself staring at often during a stop at the traffic lights, in the hands of a boy or immigrant hoping to clean your windshield for small change. Having played golf for only a short time and not being familiar with the group I didn't dare ask what it was for but understood immediately when the first player arrived with the ball about 10 meters from the flag. He used the squeegee to smooth the sand between the ball and the pole, where there was a circle of about 20 centimeters traced in the sand to represent the hole which with almost perfect putting was reached in two shots. It was an unforgettable afternoon, on the desert dunes dominating the ocean from which the wind blew refreshing us and bringing with it the scent of the sea. My fellow players gave yells of joy at every swing of the club accompanied by generous compliments from all. The complete lack of green fairways, like those back home on which they had learned to play, was totally irrelevant to everyone. The game involved passionate players who saw only the flag and flying balls, the bushes to be avoided as if they were water obstacles and where caution was taken when reclaiming balls from the long spiny plants appreciated only by the wild donkeys of the desert, who eat them daily. To avoid creating clouds of sand, that with the wind could have blinded the other golfers, everyone had tees made from rubber bands attached by a string to a wooden stick anchored in the sand, this way they didn't fly too far. Some had a small mat of synthetic grass on which they placed the ball. After a few hours of play we completed the course and returning to the cars found that the two ladies had prepared a fantastic barbeque of fish and mutton. All washed down with liters of beer and wine after which the winner of the day received a case of champagne. At the end of this fantastic day I understood that those who really love golf can play, and have a great time, in any part of the world, on any kind of terrain; with a ball that can bounce in any direction, challenging nature and its elements, putting yourself to the test, not just against your opponents but more against yourself. When I wasn't far away, because of work, in some lost oasis of the desert, we returned often to play in this or another valley on the sacred Muslim Friday; our own Sunday. During a quick visit to Italy to collect new medicines to Mauritania I also took a small golf bag, which kept me company in all my moves in the desert during the following three months that I spent in this corner of Africa. One day during a game of golf on the dunes I met Pierre, a good friend and part of the military assigned to the Belgian Ambassador. One day I was in the car with him returning to the city, we were late and the tide had already started invading the beach. We were on a street in the desert and a few kilometers from Nouakchott when we saw flashes and clouds of smoke rising above the city followed by the sound of deafening explosions. We had cars with diplomatic plates and when we arrived at an army road block an official advised us to enter the city via another road because where we were there was fighting. There was a coup in progress that the authorities were trying to contain and had instituted a curfew. There was still random rebel fire and he advised us that as soon as we reached the diplomatic area we should close ourselves in our respective embassies and not come out. I spent three days in the Belgian embassy waiting for the curfew to be lifted and calm to return to the city. This enforced cohabitation made us great friends and Pierre invited me a year later to his wedding at the Granducato in Luxembourg. I arrived a few days early and he took me to play at the Golf Club Grand Ducal where his family had been members since its founding. A very exclusive club, belonging to the royal family and headquarters, since its opening, of the European Golf Association. Signing the visitor's book I leafed through and was impressed by the number of royal and famous personalities of the international set that had played here. Golf would provide me with many more enjoyable occasions, in almost every part of the world.

NEMA

I spent the last part of my stay in Mauritania in Nema, a town (we referred to it as a shanty town) bordering Mali, where I was supposed to have set up a hospital, built by Arab countries many years before but never actually opened. Next to the empty hospital there was a large military base guarding the border. There was no television, or telephone, nothing, absolutely nothing, besides books to read that I had brought with me from Italy. After I had spent hours and hours treating patients with the strangest diseases and injuries, in order to relax a little and free my mind from the terrible situations that I had to confront, something I learned from the first days with European diplomats in Nouakchott, I planted some flags behind the fence of the hospital in an area of desert that divided the hospital from the military base. I spent an hour or so practicing golf in the desert. The second day that I played I saw a soldier arrive, who from his insignia, I recognized as an officer. It was the commanding officer of the base who had seen me playing the day before from his office. He came to inform me that I was in fact playing on the cemetery of the hospital and military base and that I could have a nasty surprise. To illustrate, he dug a hole about 20 cm deep in the sand with his hands and fragments of bone and human tissue appeared. When I asked him why there was no sign to alert people of the cemetery he told me that it was purposely unmarked to prevent grave robbers from desecrating the tombs in search of any valuable items. He invited me to enter the base saying that he had seen important personalities playing golf on TV a few times and therefore knew this sport. A short time later we planted the flags on the ground where the military carried out their exercises and I gave the first lessons to the officer, with the curious soldiers watching our every move. For two weeks, this is how my stay at Nema progressed, whenever I had some free time, I went to the military grounds to play golf with the officer, earning many lunch invitations, some clandestine beers, TV shows on the French channels, but above all the chance to call home from the telephone at the base. I don't know if the officer continued to play after I'd left for home. In any case, before I departed I left him my clubs. I was called at the end of January the year after on several days by the personnel office of my University and ordered to return immediately by order of the Foreign Ministry. I discovered that most of the finances intended for Mauritania, instead of being spent locally for humanitarian aid, where in fact being appropriated in Italy and I had the great idea, though it turned out to be useless and counterproductive, to report the fact with a fax to the director of the Cooperation Office.

I never returned to Mauritania but nostalgia for the desert has remained alive in me ever since.

THE IVORY COAST

The only vacation during those four months in Mauritania, was a week spent in the Ivory Coast with my partner who came out to meet me for New Year. We spent a few days in a Club Med village and a few more days touring the jungle. To arrive in Abidjan I had to take a plane directly from Mali, an old jet that, during the return journey appears to have crashed in the desert during a sandstorm. I had my small golf bag with me, with a few clubs, and took this opportunity to play at the Golf Club constructed next to the International Airport in the Capital. A course of 18 very nice holes, with natural, lush, subtropical vegetation. It was a shame that the humidity and heat, that easily topped 100°F, meant that I had to drink continually and also that every few minutes the deafening roar of a plane coming into land a few meters above us forced us to cover our ears and halting play for a time. At the ninth hole, exhausted from the heat, with the planes continuing overhead and cockroaches as big as sparrows climbing out of every hole I hit a ball into or even approached, but above all after we had lost so many balls in the thick rough, we finally gave up playing. The day after we were on the coast, at Club Med frequented mainly by French and Italians where the sea breeze mitigated the heat and where on a long, wide beach, helped by a local boy who followed me around, I planted a few home made flags, just outside the reserved area of the hotel and I played with the few balls I had left. After a few minutes a couple of hotel guests approached me and seeing what I was up to introduced themselves as fellow golfers. It was very entertaining to play in 5-6 holes all sharing the same clubs. I spent three days at the village. One of the golfers I met again years later when I played in the Club at Franciacorta and we followed up with an excellent lunch. One player came to meet me at my golf course. The world is so small, especially if you travel frequently. The last two days I spent crossing the jungle to reach Yamoussoukro to see the largest catholic church in the world, made as a copy of St Peter's by the then President of the Ivory Coast (rumor has it!) to ask forgiveness for all the deaths caused during his regime.

SUNNYSIDE FARM

As I have already mentioned, from 1973 I started to teach in the USA in various Universities in various States, from Florida to Wisconsin and Colorado, California and also in Canada and above all in New York at Columbia University. On average I was in North America 12 –15 times a year. Then in 1984 I was invited to hold regular courses in Atlanta. I was there 2-3 times a year for intensive Seminars on Laser Surgery. Frank Warren had signed me up to a very good contract.

It was during these years that my friend and school companion Enrico got to know about my periodic visits to Georgia for my courses, he invited me to accompany him to a farm that he had south of Atlanta. It was fantastic. I got to know a corner of the US unknown to most foreign tourists and also to many Americans themselves. Georgia, the only city in Atlanta is famous as an olympic city and also the home of Coca Cola and CNN, as well as the birthplace of Martin Luther King Jr. Most European visitors usually prefer: New York, San Francisco, Miami, and so on.

The towns close to Enrico's farm, Columbus, Buena Vista and Americus have preserved the original two floored houses, made of wood and brick, in the 1800s. Especially Americus, where on the main street the barber was eighty-two years old and still going strong, as well as cutting hair he also sold vegetables that on display inside and outside the store made for quite a show. He told me President Carter was his client. He had given up golf a couple of years before and when I went to get my hair cut this shared passion made us immediate friends. I found myself in an untouched natural setting, made up of pine trees, Georgia oaks and enormous nut trees, real forests almost impenetrable, inhabited by deer, boar, enormous fox-squirrels with long tails, armadillos and coyotes. There were enormous pastures where hundreds of cows and horses grazed, fields planted with cotton and peanuts with the classic, large plantation houses of the south characterized by large columns around the entrance, known to us from the Westerns but above all from 'Gone with the Wind'. It was just in this area that the famous film with Clark Gable and Vivien Leigh was filmed. I fell in love with this exuberant nature, with the people who, as opposed to those in New York or other famous cities, greet you on the street like a friend. When Enrico proposed that I become his partner I didn't hesitate. A couple of miles from Sunnyside Farm, there was a nine-hole golf course known to golfers in the region for its particularly technical and intriguing design. With many water obstacles, hilly terrain and woods that framed the course it was often crossed by deer and squirrels. When I saw it I had just had the first meeting with friends interested in constructing the course at La Margherita. It was 1986 and Sunnyside Farm, an hour by car from Augusta, one of the most famous courses in the world, was to become, a few years later, the starting point of a golf expedition carried out by members of the 'Girasoli Golf Club' and their friends covering the most beautiful courses in Georgia, Alabama, and Florida. Georgia and Alabama are the southern states that provided the backdrop for most of the major battles during the civil war of the middle 1800s. They are completely off the tourists route and when a Georgian meets a foreigner he immediately asks what on earth they are doing in his state. After I had traveled far and wide in the US I was struck by the population, with their warmth, the way in which they greet you as soon as your gaze meets theirs, the kindness with which they give traffic directions, often going out of their way to accompany you to areas difficult to find, which can be very useful as due to the lack of tourism there are very few sightseeing directions.

Cedar Creek Country Golf Club, a course near Sunnyside, was the first course where I played my first 9 real American holes. It was a small countryside course, nine unpretentious holes and I paid just a couple of dollars in green fees. The course was owned by Mr.Nagy, a golf professional of Hungarian origin. He had taught for years in the cold North of the US and in retirement had transferred to the fabulous climate of Georgia. His son John, also a professional (in the USA there is a profusion of professionals) with the help of a seasonal green keeper took care of the course. It was the month of June and the sun and the incredible heat had burned away most of the green, seen a few months previously, from the fairways. The course appeared to be covered in dried grass with the odd rare tuft of green and there were many areas where the sand reigned supreme. There was no need to create additional bunkers. The greens with their well tended grass were a nice blotch of color, all framed by beautiful, high stalked plants. I realized that the irrigation system served only the greens and the tees. On returning to the small club house I mentioned this fact. Old Mr. Nagy replied immediately, " in golf the most important areas are the greens and the tees, for a real golfer all the rest is optional. If you want to play on green fairways go to Callaway Gardens, you will find everything green and you'll also pay four times what you pay here" .

The second course I played, Red Oak Golf Club, about 15 miles from Sunnyside, was impossible to cover on foot due to its numerous slopes and the long distances between greens and tees. I collected a golf car to reach the first tee where other players were waiting to start. I was alone and a couple of players invited me to start with them. I noticed that in the storage box there was a huge quantity of beer and in the space under the dashboard of their car there were two pistols in their holsters. They were the sheriff of the nearby city and his deputy. When they realized that I was Italian they didn't stop asking me questions, surprised to see me in this lost area of America. They had never been out of Georgia. They were catholic and asked if I'd ever seen the pope in the flesh. They were excellent players, it was very hot and they survived by continuously drinking beer and were surprised by my refusal. I drank water and Gatorade until the 18th hole when I finally accepted a beer.

ALABAMA

Speaking of sheriffs, I was returning to Sunnyside farm with Gabriella, a friend and member of Girasoli, after a day of golf in Opelika, in the state of Alabama. I was driving along one of those large, two laned roads with an enormous, grassy area between one lane and another. The speed limit was 55 miles an hour and I was doing 70. It was late afternoon and after 18 holes, tired and hungry I couldn't wait to get home. I realized immediately that I'd just passed a police car going in the opposite direction. Checking my rearview mirror I distinctly noticed the car stopping, crossing the grassy area and giving chase with his blue and red light flashing. I slowed down, but it was too late, the car overtook me and I had to stop. A policeman got out of the car, a real sheriff, with lots of stars and a pistol on his belt. Very seriously he asked for my driving license and insurance documents. He didn't immediately realize that I was Italian, he checked the insurance and preceded in a rather brusque manner to inform me that I had exceeded the speed limit. I was ready to pay the fine when he saw my license and realized my nationality and, at the same time, noticed the golf bags. He immediately became very pleasant and asked what we were doing in Alabama and when we said that we were on vacation and that we had been playing golf he told us that he also played and had always wanted to visit Opelika but he could never find the time. He started to talk about golf, asking about golf in Italy and in the end, handing me a ticket that I took to be the usual fine he said, "this time I'll give you a warning, but pay attention because this warning will be registered in the police computer and if they catch you exceeding the limit again you'll pay double", and he let us go. Even today whenever I drive in Alabama I always respect the speed limit, thankfully this has become a little easier as recently, on the road to the golf course, they raised the limit to 70.

In 1994, Opelika, was declared by the renowned publication 'Golf Digest' as the second best public golf course in America in a ranking of 16,000 courses. In 1996, the first time that I was there I remember being struck by the fact that in the car park, most of the cars had a disabled sign.

I realized why on approaching the fabulous Club House of laminated wood, they were holding a competition for the disabled. Many of their disabilities resulted from the various wars in which the Americans have participated: Vietnam, Korea, Iraq etc. On the driving range there were disabled people with one leg or one arm, with and without prosthetics. Players keeping their balance on just one limb hitting perfect drives then returning to their crutches or wheelchairs. I was moved by their determination, with the concentration with which they practiced before setting out. I was tempted to follow the competition, to satisfy my curiosity as a player, but also as a doctor. It was enough to watch the first hole, a par four uphill where any good player would have found some difficulty, to understand how able the disabled were in confronting the challenge .

I played the 18 holes that were not in use for the tournament and to this day every time I return to Georgia, alone or with friends, I can't resist visiting and playing at that course born in Alabama at the beginning of the 1990s. The course was constructed by the local government to promote the then almost nonexistent tourism industry and stimulate the economy of a state considered, until just a few years back, the most depressed and backward in the US. Trent Jones, one of the most famous golf architects, planned and realized seven golf complexes in a short time, spread around the state, creating a total of over 300 holes. In the successive years, these attracted more than a million golfers from every part of the world, especially Japan, to little known Alabama. This took the local authorities by surprise, not having considered the hotel infrastructure they found themselves in difficulty dealing with all these unexpected guests. Only after a few years, in this beautiful golf complex, placed into the perfect untouched natural environment, were any hotels built. Unfortunately, these did not in any way respect their environment (the Marriot Hotel for example). The hotels were built from enormous blocks of cement reminiscent of funeral homes, in no way welcoming or in keeping with their beautiful surroundings. I remember, following a long day of golf under the relentless sun with some friends, tired and soaking with sweat, we decided to stay a night at the adjacent hotel as there were no showers or changing rooms in the clubhouse. The hotel foyer was so cold (not least because of the usual excessive air conditioning) that we preferred to suffer a long journey home in the car, rather than stay in this amorphous block of cement.

PIT AND ALLEN

I n 1992, as well as having just started to play golf at the new Club Girasoli, I was still skiing, flying ultralight planes and taking long rides on my horse. During one of these solitary rides, with my old Solange, a bardigiano horse that had accompanied me on dozens of trips in our neighboring Alps, I found myself crossing Val Troncea, on a splendid summer day. Unexpectedly, I saw in the distance someone who looked as though he were playing golf. He was quite a distance away and I couldn't be sure that he really was playing or just doing something similar to a golf swing. I got closer and could see that, in fact, it really was a young golfer. I stopped a few hundred meters from him, observing with keen interest. I knew that in this area no golf course of any kind existed and was curious to see what he was up to. He had two irons and a wood that he kept in one hand resting them on his back. He took 4 or 5 balls from the pocket of his trousers, he put them in a row on the ground, about 20 centimeters distance from each other and hit them one after another, after positioning himself facing a tree about 100 meters away. I was not capable, at this point, of judging his swing, but it appeared to me that he moved well. The balls went straight in the direction of the tree. I discretely approached Pit, this was the name of the boy, at the base of a pine tree in the middle of the roots that spread around the ground. I was fascinated by the spectacle. He collected the balls and prepared his club to take the next shots towards a tree further away. In this way he came in my direction. He was shocked to see me jump out behind him. We introduced ourselves and I complimented him on the nice shots that I'd just witnessed. I climbed down from my horse, tied Solange to a bush and accompanied him for a few 'holes', chatting together. He told me that he'd seen a lot of golf on TV and had fallen in love with the sport. He also explained that the father of one of his school mates was a tenacious golfer. He wanted his son to learn golf from an early age, insisting that he follow him on the course every Sunday. At a certain age the boy preferred to play football and ski and decided to abandon the sport to his father. The friend knew that Pit was passionate about golf and he'd donated some of his clubs and taught him the rudimentaries of the swing. His family were of limited means and he couldn't afford the fees at a Club and, therefore, his passion led him to play in the middle of the forest in the Val Troncea, where his parents frequently went for their Sunday picnic.

He was 17 and so contented with his golf experience, He spoke with such enthusiasm that I invited him to come and play at my club giving him an annual membership.

This episode reminds me of another, that of a young black man who I met at a public Golf course in Atlanta a short while after. I noticed him making a few shots on the driving range. When I took the car to the first tee I found him waiting for me. He introduced himself as Allen and asked if he could play with me. I was alone and more than happy to agree to his request. He would keep me company. He put his bag into the car taking out a driver. After I'd made my shot, I invited him to make his, he made a few practice swings asking, "could you take a look at my swing and let me know if it's ok?". This made me smile, as a newcomer to golf I didn't feel that I was the best person to judge his swing and I told him so. He responded candidly, "among those that I saw on the driving range I liked your swing best and for this reason I chose you to play with". I thanked him for the compliment and thanked my instructor Peter from the heart. Allen was 12, his father didn't play golf and was not at all interested in this sport. He was a fan of Tiger Wood, who had just started to have success and was considered a prodigy. We set off and he confided in me immediately that every morning on the weekends, when he was free from school, he arrived early to help collect the balls from the driving range. He also helped with other small duties. In exchange he was allowed to train and play for free. He had no money for lessons and a golf bag with clubs of various brands, made up of those found or lost on the course and never reclaimed. At this public course there were no instructors and he'd learned by observing other players on the driving range, day after day, following any advice that other players wanted to give him. When he was on the course he selected a solitary player like myself, to play 18 holes and hopefully to receive some useful advice. That day he chose me. I was rather flattered and gave my all to teach him something, repeating many of the things that Peter always told me. That day I lost a lot of balls and each time Allen gave me some more saying that he had hundreds, found on the course. At the end of the course I invited him to eat a hamburger or a hotdog, the only food available at the small club house. As I was leaving he presented me with a water pitcher from a famous club in Atlanta.

On many American courses I've seen kids of various ages, some playing with their parents who teach their children the first steps of golf, others alone who self learn, just like Allen. I've often asked American professionals about this and all of them, without exception, have referred to it as common practice for most American parents to personally start their children playing golf and then continue to follow them afterwards. "Unfortunately only the parents that can really afford it turn to a professional for their children's' first lessons," continuing that," "the others are given a teacher only if they are particularly gifted or show promise towards becoming a champion".

GOA

The Indian region of Goa has never been particularly famous for its golf courses. Even today it has few courses, except for a few luxury hotels that understand how this sport can attract new clients. The Portuguese dominion has not in the past favored the sport, instead it is more popular in the Indian regions populated by the English. I was on vacation in Goa, I had just arrived at Calangute beach, and tired, after spending a few hours on the beach I abandoned my friends and went off to make a tour inland. Half hidden by the branches of a tree, I saw a sign indicating 'Golf Club'. Taking a dirt path that, after a few hundred meters, took me to a wooden cottage, in front of which were parked a couple of cars, and a rail on which to rest golf bags. I entered and found a small reception, with a very kind young Indian lady who greeted me with a bow and asked me if I'd like to play. It was midday and the heat was rather too suffocating to accept the invitation. I asked if I could take a look at the course and she asked me to take the door facing the rear. I found myself in a beautiful tropical garden of dense vegetation where the fairways were covered with the kind of grass that I'd only seen in the Ivory Coast. What really hit me were the greens, instead of being green were grey-black standing out in the middle of all that greenery. I approached the final hole of the course that was a few meters from the Club house and could see that instead of grass the greens were, in fact, made of smoothed earth like that of a tennis court. There were no golfers here but I could see a couple in the distance. I returned to the reception where in the meantime two Indian golfers had arrived. The lady presented the golfers, members of the board of the Club, to me and knowing that I was Italian and president of a club they wanted to offer me a beer and invited me to play with them. I turned the offer down, though I made myself available for the next day, but still asked about their course. It was founded a few years previously by a group of English people who worked in the region. There were a few local members of the club but the number of players was rather small, and they couldn't manage to finance the running of a full course. The most economic solution had been the choice of greens made of smoothed earth that required almost no maintenance and with just one man and one grass cutting machine pulled by an old tractor to cut the fairways, they had in practice resolved the problem. The running costs could be easily covered by membership fees together with the green fees from players passing through. To dispel any doubts I might have about the quality of the course they insisted that I attempt an approach in order to test the perfect impact on its surface. I must admit that the ball landed in exactly the same way as on the best greens that I've played and my two Indian companions told me that the secret was all in the irrigation. For putting, they confessed that you had to get used to the ground, but that this problem applied to all players who were used to other surfaces. The next day, late afternoon, when the heat had abated a little I found the two Indians waiting for me. They had brought along another player, their friend, because he was also a surgeon. At the first hole I had some difficulty on the first green, but soon I got used to putting harder and found the right measure required to reach at the hole. My Indian colleagues knew that I was staying just a few days and wanted to invite me to their home for lunch together with their family and after they had insisted for some time I felt obliged by courtesy to accept. It turned out to be an eye-opener to life in a household of this high social class. We were about twenty around a large table for lunch. The Indian tradition is that the male sons live, together with their families, with their father on whose death the oldest son becomes the new head of the household. My colleagues first introduced me to their wives and then one by one to the six sons with their respective wives, some of whom were busy preparing lunch in a nearby kitchen. Some children, the older ones, ate lunch together with us in a disciplined manner, while the smaller children, even though they had their own chairs, moved about all over the place taking handfuls of food from the plates of their various fellow diners. I noticed that no-one reprimanded them, when they came close to me hesitating for a moment, looking at me with their splendid eyes and, having taken stock, reaching out their hands to steal a handful of food from my plate before rushing off quickly. The head of the household, who must have noticed my surprise, informed me that it was the habit in many families such as theirs to leave the children free to move around and act as they liked until the age of five, after which they were given to teachers who educated them very strictly for their future lives. The day after I left for the Indi University at Varanasi, in the old city of santa di Benares.

KENYA THE WINDSOR GOLF CLUB

If you ever go to Nairobi don't miss the opportunity to play at the Windsor Golf Club. From the name you realize immediately the obvious English origin and the splendid clubhouse along with the style of the cottages found along the fairway of the first hole confirm this.

In the office, where I introduced myself as the Chairman of my Club, the director immediately invited me to consider myself a guest of the Club, he accompanied me to the bar offering me a beer, inviting me to participate in a competition the next day organized by journalists from Nairobi. I thanked him but I was, unfortunately, obliged to refuse as the next day I was leaving on a Safari in the Serengeti.

At the first tee the Caddy master entrusted me to Ernest, my Caddy and asked if I also required a 'Flower caddy'. I didn't want to appear too ignorant so I didn't dare ask what this could be but, assuming that it was a question of a few shillings, I said yes and we started.

While I was preparing for my swing with a couple of warm up exercises, the 'Flower caddy' walked to an area about 150-200 meters from the tee while his companion gave me some suggestions on the direction to which I should make my drive. I hit a decent drive which sent my ball almost two hundred meters to the border of the first rough and immediately understood the purpose of the 'flower caddy'. He ran to the area where my ball had landed, searching he found it and positioned it next to a flower picked from the side of the fairway, so that on my arrival I would immediately see it and could continue without delay. The same sequence was repeated in continually, every time I lost a ball in the rough or on the fairway where the grass was particularly high. With my second shot I managed to clear the edge of the rough and directly ahead I saw a spectacle that I couldn't identify immediately. It took me a few seconds before I realized that in the middle of the fairway, about 200 meters away, there was a row of round female bottoms, I could see about twenty ladies bent over. Ernest informed me that they were the ladies who worked to weed the grass of undesirable vegetation. The golf course was in a natural park where the use of any type of chemical product was absolutely prohibited; therefore, all undesirable weeds on the course, fairways, greens, tees, are eliminated manually.

My caddy whistled, the head of the group responded by waving all the ladies to the side of the fairway and then gave us the sign that I could continue with my game. A little preoccupied, in case I made a mistake and hit the ladies, I messed up my shot and sent the ball to the edge of the forest. And here there was a surprise waiting for me, two monkeys appeared out of the trees took my ball threw it at each other in the middle of the fairway. The ladies in the meantime who had broken out in laughter, becoming animated, patting each other on the back and looking at me with a certain amusement.

I followed the monkeys that appeared almost as if they'd been trained: they looked at me a short time and then at the ladies, then suddenly with a final throw hurled the ball into the middle of the legs of the ladies and disappeared back into the forest.

I didn't understand if the caddy was taking me for a ride or not. He told me that as the monkeys are considered a natural obstacle, I must play the shot from where it landed after being thrown. I found myself, therefore, surrounded by about twenty ladies who, with a couple of words of English mixed with Swahili, encourage me with my next shot. "Hakuna matata sir" they repeated whilst smiling. I noticed that the group was made up of ladies of every age amongst which a few young and very beautiful girls stood out. The most daring, or should I say, disinhibited, were those of middle age, who laughed continually, calling me to make my shot.

I found out later that they work 8 to 10 hours a day for a few shillings, plus meals for the day, and food that they are given to take home. Obviously, surrounded by all these ladies constantly laughing, despite my caddy's pleas for silence, I made another mistake that sent the ball skidding just a few meters away. At this point the head of the group and Ernest, speaking in their dialect, started exchanging what seemed to be insults. Suddenly the group became silent and I manage to make a decent shot which took me close to the green. A splendid green, perfectly groomed, where the ball rolls forward without ever deviating from its initial direction.

There were others surprises to follow the monkeys, antelope that crossed the course, snakes that my caddy removed from the fairway without hesitation, lifting them with pieces of wood, and placing them on the edge of the fairway or directly into the forest. I expected to see a lion appear any moment or another dangerous animal but my caddy calmed my overactive imagination.

In contrast to the course in the Ivory Coast cockroaches didn't crawl out of the holes and when I spoke to Ernest, he took the cup out of the hole and gave it to me to smell, there was a strange rather acrid smell and he told me that they sprayed a natural liquid into the holes that kept the insects away, cockroaches, scorpions, snakes and a whole host of other beasts that it's best to avoid direct contact with.

When two of my balls landed deep in the forest, Ernest immediately told me that it would be impossible to find them. The maintenance of the course is limited only to the course itself and nothing outside of it is touched. In the forest the vegetation is so thick that to enter you need to work hard with a machete and electric saw in order to penetrate the vegetation. And this is not to mention the risk of meeting the various undesirables hiding there. From the smile which accompanied his offer of some balls taken from his pocket I thought that the forest must be their hunting reserve for balls during their free time. They probably collected all the lost balls and then offer them back to the players who obviously pay for them or leave a small tip. On every shot Ernest gave me precious advice, and I soon realized that he was a good player, much better than myself. He corrected my sight and showed me the defects in my swing, giving me advice like an instructor.

After a few holes my game, thanks to him, had improved a lot and when, thanking him for his advice, I drew his attention to the fact I was hitting much further than usual, he very modestly drew my attention to the fact that this could be due to the altitude in Nairobi.

Re-entering the clubhouse I had the pleasant surprise of finding the Vice-president of the Club waiting for me. He was an old, retired English diplomat. He had been in Italy a number of times, playing courses in Rome and Venice, and was hoping to return as soon as possible as he missed the Mediterranean cuisine. He immediately mentioned Costantino Rocca who he knew and who on occasion he'd had dinner with after a competitions.

He had already seen on the internet the site of La Margherita and the

Girasoli. He already knew all about me and my course. He invited me for dinner and I was forced to make another refusal. I had friends waiting at the Safari Hotel. I promised that when I returned to the Serengeti I'd be in touch, something that I couldn't honor and for which I excused myself once back in Italy thanking him for his hospitality and inviting him to Italy.

I would never see him again, but I will always remember his kindness and above all the Windsor Golf Club, considered, the star of African golf clubs.

The following year I returned to Kenya, and Malindi. A naive friend, convinced me to sign a contract with a Roman company and invest in a time share property. I accepted when I found out that there was a nine hole course nearby. One arrival I realized that I'd been taken for a ride and that the much extolled villas on the sea shore didn't exist.

It was high season and we went around the hotels, without finding one suitable, until we arrived at the White Elephant: completely full. The taxi driver had unloaded our bags among which was my golf bag. While we were deciding what to do, we saw a beautiful couple approaching: she, wide eyed, tall and beautiful, the figure of a model and tanned, talking to her companion, Dario, even more tanned that her, lots of hair, with an easy going and likeable look. They were speaking with a strong Piedmont accent. Passing by she remarked to Dario " look at that nice bag".

I took this opportunity to ask if they played golf, unfortunately they didn't play, but in any case we introduced ourselves. We discovered that we were from the same part of Piedmont and that Dario's mother knew my mother. Dario's companion told us that, working in fashion and specifically furs, she very much admired my leather golf bag of the 'Trent Jones Golf ' brand bought in Opelika.

How small the world really is and how a golf bag can provoke such a favorable meeting. We explained to them our bad luck with the time share property and our fruitless search for lodgings. No problem: Ombretta and Dario were leaving for Italy. The meeting had been providential. They had a fantastic villa on the beach, next to the hotel. They took us there, introduce us to the girl who cleaned and who was just closing the house , they left us the key and with best wishes for a nice stay they left promising to get in touch when we were all in Italy. Meetings that would be repeated in the coming years as we become friends.

MALINDI

M alindi, seaside city on the Indian Ocean, with huge beaches, especially when the tide goes out, holiday destination of the Italians, hiding place of criminals on the run, a few miles from the border with Somalia, often crossed by raiders to reach inland cities to make their attacks. Large hotels, many villas, holiday homes, a beautiful African market full of spices and a golf course.

I know that today the situation has improved. The course has 11 holes with decent greens, 15 tees and a new clubhouse. Many years ago, I encountered a bungalow with a small bar and a girl at reception. When I paid the green fee asking for some information about the course the secretary told me that at the first tee there were two Italian players who were members of the Club. If I could catch up with them I could play with them and that they knew the course very well and could provide all the information I required. That's how I got to know Sandro and his wife. A delightful old couple. When I told them that I'd played at the Windsor Golf Club in Nairobi they smile and said that I would certainly have to adapt to a very uneven course where the ball on impact with the ground goes all over the place and hardly ever in the desired direction and that above all you have to learn how to select the correct club.

I immediately notice the difference. The fairways were, in essence, of clay with the odd oasis of dry grass. There was no irrigation system; this was left to the rainy season.

Onto the first green Sandro used a putter, from the fairway, from a distance of almost 40 meters and the ball zigzagged along the intended line and stopped, to my amazement, close to the flag. I understood his game when, attempting an approach with a pitching wedge, the club crashed against the hard, dry ground, bouncing back to hit the ball, making it fly as if I'd used a driver.

On the greens the only green area was a small 2 to 3 meter circle around the hole with all the rest completely dry. I realized why, when at the next hole I saw a worker watering, the area under the flag with a watering can. Taking water from a small metal bin on a trolley. I lear-ned immediately that the putter was the most important club to use, with the correct force you could reach a green even from 100 meters away, while the other clubs could only be used on the rare areas of dried grass.

After just 4 or 5 holes I'd learned how you needed to move and play on this surface, thanks to advice from Sandro and his wife. Also here just like at Windsor the monkeys reigned supreme, running across the fairways, though without stopping to collect balls. While playing I'd seen some cows eating a strip of grass at the edge of the course, but when we arrived at the last hole, which was a little bit greener, we saw a colored man, at our arrival, shoving away a young calf which had been quietly grazing on the final green. What a huge difference from the Windsor Golf, you could say "from the stars to the stalls".

Sitting at a table in the small bar, sipping a beer, Sandro told me how for 20 years he had been a seasonal resident of Malindi spending at least six months of the year, from Autumn to Spring and how on his arrival in Africa he had discovered that the local climate had rid him of all the rheumatic pain from which he had suffered for years. He immediately invited me to dinner, when he realized that I didn't have a car he told his wife to give me the key to theirs. Seeing my discomfort he informed me, "we are 200 meters from the golf club and we have two cars, you can easily keep it for the remainder of your stay".

In the evening we found ourselves in an enormous villa shaped like a horseshoe, with a roof of makuti and a large pool, a myriad of person-nel and a security guard. Sandro was a builder. His company had just finished building the new headquarters of the Deutsche Bank in Ber-lin, after the wall fell, and he was building dams in Africa and South America. His children worked in the company and he could, therefore, spend long periods in Africa. We played often together in those two weeks and we were often his dinner guests. When I returned to Italy in Spring, I managed to return his hospitality by hosting him a number of times at my club.

The following year we returned to Malindi and he insisted on hos-ting us at his home. This is how I discovered that, in all the years spent in Africa, he had adopted tens of orphaned children, allowing them to study. Some of the children had even graduated and among these he was proud to introduce me to one who had graduated in medicine in

Italy. Now I understood why in Malindi, the locals when speaking of him refer to father Sandro.

CRANS KITZBUHEL (Ugo and Gabi)

A few years ago I was in Switzerland, in Crans sur Sierre, for an acupuncture congress. Close to our hotel there was a famous Swiss golf course, with a fabulous clubhouse and the most beautiful fairways on a mountain course that I have ever played on. With a marvelous and priceless view of Mont Blanc and the Matterhorn, the two highest alpine peaks and most recognized in the Alps. The final afternoon of my stay, with the congress finished, I arrived at the course to play nine holes, before the sun set at this the beginning of summer. I was playing alone and after a short time reached a couple of players who had been ahead by a couple of holes. They invited me to join them and I got to know Ugo and Gabi, a lovely couple with their dog who followed them very obediently without leaving their side and without disturbing anyone. We played the final holes with the dog that seemed to watch every shot, tempted to chase the ball, but resisting and above all without ever hampering the game. His owners had trained him very well. At the end of the round we sat down at the nineteenth hole to drink an aperitif, chatting and getting acquainted. Ugo was part of the press covering the Olympic Games and when he heard that I lived close to Turin, where shortly the winter games would be taking place, he asked my advice on lodgings in the area. He was very fond of camper holidays and was searching for a campsite or something of that type. What could be better than a golf course like Girasoli, with its attached holiday farm and bar. The next year Ugo, Gabi and their dog arrived with their camper at Girasoli where they stayed, not just for the Olympic Games, but for years and they are to this day seasonal guests of our club. I remember the golf club at Crans not just for the very demanding course, but more, the fabulous panorama surrounding the course. A landscape similar to, even if the peaks weren't quite as high, to that I'd seen the previous year in Austria when I played around the pastures of Kitzbuhel. Here there was always the risk of hitting a cow quietly grazing on the course and the greens were protected by a small electric fence, that was easy to climb over, from any possible cow invasion at the collar. I played with an Austrian friend who quoted the local rules to me, including one that I remember very well was the obligation to drop the ball at least half a meter away when it landed next to or in a cowpat to "avoid the undesirable risk of finishing covered," he quoted word for word, "in cow shit". Years later I was reminded of this rule when playing on the pastures of Georgia. As you could also say here **"from the stars to the stalls."**

LOS ANGELES

I was leading a seminar in laser surgery for the treatment of cutaneous angiomas, those disfiguring red specks known as 'spider angioma'. I'd been invited to Los Angeles by Roger, a famous cosmetic surgeon, who I'd got to know at another congress in New York. Roger had appreciated my work and was very interested for his own activities. Among his clients were some of the most famous faces in Hollywood history. He invited me to dinner one evening with his wife in a place that was the regular haunt of many actors and actresses and he introduced me to a couple of them. I remember Demi Moore and others, but also others, less famous whose names I can't recall. Chatting about my work we realized that we were both keen golfers and he automatically invited me to play at his Club. This was a Country Golf Club, 18 holes, very exclusive, where the membership was limited to three hundred and members could invite, for free, no more than five guests per year. I was the fourth that year. Two days later and I found myself about half an hour outside Los Angeles at an enormous Farm with attached Golf and Country Club. The clubhouse was one of the most luxurious that I'd every seen, even if later on I would have similar experiences. I was presented to a number of members and they all told me that I was one of the very few Italians that had played on their course and they were very shocked when I confessed that at the hospital where I worked, among the hundreds of doctors. we numbered no more that twenty who played golf. At this club doctors were very well represented and made up a large percentage of the membership.

I was very worried about the immense heat, but my worries immediately vanished when I climbed into the golf car and was bowled over by a jet of air arriving from two very efficient fans. Behind our seats there was a beautifully displayed small fridge containing drinks of every type. "Fringe benefits for members and their guests," Roger informed me. Despite the air conditioning, the heat and the activity (I walked beside the car), made us sweat and drink intensely and after a couple of holes we'd finished all there was to drink. Everything seemed to be perfectly organized because, as we finished the last bottle, a service car with a splendid girl arrived behind us and she refilled our fridge with cold drinks. I drank only water and Gatorade, Roger to my horror downed beer after beer. The course was beautiful but very flashy, between various fairways there were, let's say, natural works of art, created by a garden architect in collaboration with the designer of the golf course. Fountains with cascades, Pompeii style, with a myriad of exotic flowers, bushes with a mosaic of different colored flowers picture perfect, but the thing that really struck me was a hill about ten meters high in the form of an Egyptian pyramid, all covered with a grassy mantle that was perfectly trimmed. Just at the moment we were passing alongside the top of the pyramid a sprinkler popped up shining in the sun and, with a beautiful water display sprayed the grassy mantle below. I wondered how they managed to cut a hedge at such a step angle. "Very easy", responded a companion, "by hand". As we were playing on a green I heard a small noise that immediately caused Roger to tell me to move over to the side, the sprinkler system started up and sprayed the green for a couple of minutes. The whole course was equipped with a system of sensors that measured the level of humidity from zone to zone setting into action the sprinklers, which often also watered the players who hadn't heard the small warning sound but who during the hottest parts of the day certainly appreciated the service. The car was equipped with GPS, often on American courses this really helped during the game, not only providing us with the exact distance required for our shot, but also providing valuable advice for the choice of club. On our return to the clubhouse, a little confused from the heat and amazement at the course and its services, between one drink and another I asked Roger about the membership fees for the Club and when he told me I wondered just how much members must earn. It seemed that he'd read my mind. Practically it cost them nothing, he continued, and he explained how at the end of each year he and his accountant went to negotiate with the tax office on his financial situation the following year. The relationship was very clear. If the tax office accepted the deductible expenses, not only for the golf membership but also the expenses of his boat that he kept at the sailing club, activities that he declared were indispensable for his relaxation and therefore linked to his ability to work and earn more, he could earn and pay taxes on tens of millions of dollars, with expenses deductible. In another case you could be limited to earning half the specific amount and therefore pay a lot less tax. The tax office, having made the relevant calculations, always accepted. My colleague Bob

Saporiti, a New York dentist, told me almost the same thing. It would be great if the Italian financial system followed this example, without a doubt they would earn double from Italian professionals and entrepreneurs and also service suppliers whose earnings would not escape the auditors.

AUGUSTA

R oger's cousin, the Manager of Sunny Side Farm, was one of the many seasonal green keepers at the mythical Augusta course. On this course some of the most important tournaments in the United States are held and it's impossible for a normal golfer to play there. According to urban myth many of the presidents of the USA have been refused permission to play. The prestigious American publication Golf Digest describes it, not as a Golf course, but like a TV set providing the backdrop for the numerous programmes that transmit the most important tournaments taking place there. I realized later just how true this definition is.

I was very surprised when, almost by accident, as I was speaking with Roger about my course and some maintenance problems we were having he told me that I could ask some advice from his cousin Mark, who lived a little more than an hour from Sunny Side. I invited him for dinner one evening. I already knew that it was impossible to play at Augusta but I was very curious to take a look. But I knew that this was also very difficult. You had to know one of the management staff, but Mark insisted that, with some prior notice, it could be arranged. And sure enough at dawn a couple of days later, before the sun had shown its face, but with the light of the moon still visible, Mark gave me a green keeper's uniform to wear and he introduced me to the course, before the course staff arrived. We climbed on a works vehicle and started the tour. The first thing I noticed were the greens that, on the TV, always appeared to be surrounded by vegetation of every kind, small bushes and tall plants with and without flowers. The tall plants were there as expected but the small bushes were missing and in their place were empty spaces where they should have been. Mark took me to an enormous greenhouse where I saw hundreds of plants in flower. He told me that the weather could change from one day to another, even within a couple of hours. Cold winds from the north could arrive unexpectedly, which would have damaged many of the plants and for this reason the most delicate and more importantly, the tropical plants full of flowers, were kept and nurtured in the greenhouse, and were put on show on the course only during tournaments. Many greens were almost completely covered in sand and others with plastic sheets. I was very disappointed, by the pastel green color of the fairways, Mark told me that a few days before they had "painted" the grass that had been a little burned by one of the cold winds from the north. The tour lasted a short time, less than an hour, to avoid the workers who would be arriving shortly.

The Golf Digest journalists were completely right.

ICELAND

O n this island in the extreme north of Europe the speed limit is 40 km an hour. Those who've never been there can't possibly understand the reason, but when you arrive you immediately understand why. The Island is the size of Northern Italy or just one of the North American states, gathered on this land are sights and marvels of nature that one can only see elsewhere by visiting many different countries in various part of the world. Here are some of the largest glaciers in the world, also many volcanoes, small and large, always grumbling or erupting. When I was there for the first time, a small distance from the coast, a whole island was destroyed by the eruptions and the inhabitants were rapidly evacuated, without any major tragedies, these things happen all the time here. At the sides of many streets you often see signs warning, "danger erupting volcanoes". Earthquakes are an everyday occurrence and along the way you can admire enormous geysers periodically sending their clouds of hot water and vapor towards the sky. The land trembles and it's pointless to tar the streets, the ground is constantly in movement. To exceed 40 km is almost impossible and whoever tries risks careering off the road at any moment. Traveling through deserts of sand, rocks or covered with moss, you can suddenly find yourself in front of a miniature Niagara falls or alongside a small Grand Canyon and you can walk on the beaches of the blackest volcanic sand. But away from the wild areas where nature can play some nasty tricks, you will often find yourself in huge green meadows inhabited by hundreds of sheep and small Icelandic ponies.

Of about 300,000 inhabitants, 130,000 live spread out around the island in small groups and it's easy to see, on arrival in these villages, a small arrow indicating 'Golf course'. With a golfing history of little over 50 years, today one person in six plays golf and the number of players is estimated to be between 40,000 and 50,000. Nature has favored the Icelandic meadows covered in a rich and incredibly thick, grassy mantle, where during summer, with 24 hours of light, a sparkling sun in a clear, unpolluted sky and a particularly dry climate, it's possible to cut the grass and collect the hay perfectly dried in the same day. It's in these meadows that the inhabitants of the small Icelandic villages carve out their 6 or 9 hole golf courses, using the same machine, modifying the height for three different cuts, one for the fairway, one for the collar and the last for the greens. Some of these holes are completely surrounded by the classic electric fences used for animals (sheep and ponies) that quietly graze at the sides of the fairway, considered to be the rough and where it isn't recommended to hit the ball as you'll never be able to find it. At other courses, only the greens have this protection, like in Kitzbuhel.

In Reykjavik, one afternoon, I tried to book a tee off for the next morning on a 18 hole course and I was candidly informed that the first tee off time available for the next day was at midnight. Unfortunately, as I had to leave I couldn't play, but I was allowed to visit the course. The fairways were perfectly trimmed surrounded by hills of volcanic rock in a fabulous environment on the edge of the sea. At every hole there were groups of five or more people among them many children and entire families. There wasn't a hole free of players and on the tee of one hole, other groups were waiting to start. With only a few months of light, and few months without snow, the local golfers had to make the most of the very limited time available.

On the day of my departure from the island, I had a car adventure similar to the one in Alabama. After 10 days driving on dirt roads, Close to Reykjavik, I unexpectedly found myself on an asphalt road. It was, as I found out shortly after, a road with a coating of experimental elastic asphalt, intended to test its resistance to the continual underground movements. It seemed too good to be true, carried away by the speed and after many days driving at 40 km an hour, I accelerated to 100 km per hour. I'd covered a couple of kilometers when I met a police car that turned around to follow and stop me. A very polite policeman approached the car, looked at the passengers, my friend Oscar and my son Francesco sleeping on the back seat with his mother. He invited me to follow him with all my documents to the police car, where he had me sit on the back seat and locked the doors. Checking my documents he asked who the other passengers were and what my plans were. I replied that we had been going to the airport, where we would be leaving in a few hours, to return to Italy. He explained in front of the other police officers that on this stretch of road, even though asphalted, the speed limit was still 40 km/hr and he started to speak into his radio. Putting down the microphone he asked me to wait patiently and started to chat with the other officers. After a few minutes waiting my wife came to see what was going on and tried unsuccessfully to open the door. The police informed her that they couldn't open the door as I was actually under arrest. I asked for an explanation and they very kindly informed me that the speed limit was 40 km/hr but up to 70 km /hr there was a sliding scale of fines applicable but that above 70 m/hr immediate arrest was standard. They should have taken me to prison and the day after to court, where a judge would have sanctioned the punishment. Having seen my small son with his mother and knowing that we should be returning to Italy that evening they were trying to find, via radio, the chief of police to ask for instructions. But he could not be found. I was, therefore, required to wait patiently for a final decision. After half an hour the chief of police called the officers who explained the case. At the end of the conversation the doors of the car were unlocked and the police gave me my documents saying that I could go. When I asked about a possible fine, they replied that for this speed there was no designated fine but only immediate arrest and that they didn't want to be mean to a tourist with his family and they were letting me go. But they added, " the next time you come here, remember that you are on file and that even for a relatively minor offence you will be arrested and taken in front of a judge".

When I returned a few years later I always insisted that my friends drove.

FLORIDA (THE ALLIGATORS)

F lorida is famous for its magnificent golf courses but also for the alligators that you find, usually in small numbers but all over the place.

Very often in the lakes that you find on a golf courses you see signs with, " beware of the alligators" to alert players who are searching for the odd ball that fell into the water. Generally these alligators are small and don't present any real danger, but in some cases they have bitten ball collectors, who were busy collecting the thousands of balls that fall every year into the lakes of golf courses, fortunately without grave consequences. I have personally assisted on one of these occasions on such a golf course, when a player, determined to recover his ball from the edge of a lake had the ball snatched from his hand, and jumping backwards fell to the ground, standing up quickly and running away in fear that the alligator would climb out to bite him. In these private golf clubs when I arrived alone I was asked to wait for another solitary golfer as it was prohibited to set off alone in a golf car. At the beginning of the first hole there was a small queue of players waiting and you had to arrive almost half an hour before tee off time in order to begin. Finally the Master of the course who managed the tee offs, informed me, smiling towards the car park, that I would be able to set off almost immediately, as a club member, alone like me, had just arrived. When I turned to see the new arrival I saw a gentleman of a distinguished age who was parking a bike that he'd just dismounted. Behind the saddle, held by a special harness, I saw a sack containing six or seven clubs. The Master introduced us and we set off. My companion was over 80 years old and lived more than 15 miles from the golf club. Almost every day he left home on his bike to arrive at the course and play a game. He was in perfect physical shape and looked at least 15 years younger. He immediately asked if I'd be willing to bet a couple of dollars per hole, insisting that if there wasn't something at stake he wouldn't be able to fully engage in the game. I didn't know how he played, but as it involved just a few dollars, I accepted. He was a great player and at the end of the 18 holes I'd lost about 50 dollars.

He offered me a drink at the end of the game and later climbed on his bike to return home. I followed him slowly for a couple of miles returning to my hotel and I saw him disappear off into the distance.

CROATIA - THE BRIJUNI ISLANDS

T he Brijuni Islands, in the northern Adriatic, once part of the Austrian-Hungarian empire, were acquired by the Viennese magnate Kupelwieser, at the end of the 1800s to create a luxurious tourist centre. With this in mind, following the construction of a large hotel in 1922, an 18 hole golf course was created, designed by two famous architects of the time. This was the course on which for a number of years, the first Adriatic Open was played. The most famous golfers from all over Europe and also the distant USA participated in the open. The course was considered one of the most beautiful courses in southern Europe.

The ambitious tourist project unfortunately failed, to the extent that the owner took his own life and the complex was bought by the Italian state that converted it into a military base. Immediately after the second world war the island was taken over by Yugoslavia and became the preferred residence of the President, Marshal Tito, who hosted over 100 heads of state and famous stars of the cinema there. There was a large zoo on the island, populated by many wild animals presented to Tito, for his passion for hunting.

By strange coincidence I visited the islands of Brijuni in 1967 and saw the golf course from a distance. A few years before, freshly graduated, I had examined a Yugoslavian guest staying in a large Turin Hotel suffering from renal colic. I administered a drip with drugs and waited for the pain to subside. When I saw him again a few hours later, the pain had passed and he wanted to pay me for my treatment. I told him that I considered him a guest in my country and despite his insistence, I refused payment. He left the next day to return home and before he left he asked if I was a hunter. He wanted to give me his business card in case I visited Yugoslavia one day. On the card I could only make out the name "Peru Trotin", the rest written in Slavic was totally incomprehensible to me.

At the time I was a big fan of hunting, capable of following a herd of deer in the mountains, for days, in the rain, sleeping in the open, together with my three hunting companions Teulin the smuggler, Dreino the truck driver and Notu, the forester. Three years later I was invited, by a friend, to hunt turtle doves in the Yugoslav countryside of Novi Sad, where these birds had become a real scourge to agriculture, destroying, in just a few hours, entire plantations of sunflowers and every other cultivable cereal. After two days of hunting and having fired more than a thousand shots, one evening I remembered the promise made and found the business card in my wallet to call the mysterious patient cured years before. Imagine my surprise when I discovered from the hunting guide accompanying me that day that Mr. Peru Trotin was not just a good friend and companion of Tito's but also responsible for all the hunting in Yugoslavia, at the time the main source of foreign currency, equivalent to an important ministry of finance. The day after we were hunting, for free, in a large reserve on the outskirts of Novi Sad. Two days later, Peru Trotin took us to Brijuni, the private reserve of Marshal Tito, to hunt for large African ducks. One day sitting on a boat in the middle of a swamp, while trying to retrieve a recently shot goose from the water, I became entangled and my watch strap broke. The watch fell to the depths and Peru Trotin took from his wrist his magnificent steel Zenith and insisted on presenting it to me.

That evening we ate and passed the night in a grand old hotel. We should have a spent a few days on the islands, but unexpectedly they announced the arrival of Tito and we had to leave. Shortly before we left Peru Trotin, accompanying us to the port, took us to the golf course that was partially abandoned, where I noted the greens were made of pressed white sand. Thirty years later with a Croatian friend, during a summer vacation in Istria, I returned to Brijuni and played on those greens. The course had never had an irrigation system and was watered only by natural precipitation. The fairways were a bit dry, the greens were still constructed of sand and we enjoyed ourselves immensely. I know that the course was completely renovated in 2006 – but I have yet to inspect it!

CUBA

At the beginning of the 1990's Cuba, after a long period of isolation, launched tourism in order to help resolve the economic situation on the island. With a couple of friends we spent a few weeks on the outskirts of Havana, before they began restoration work there. Many houses and the cathedral, parts of a once splendid city, were partly in ruins, very much abandoned, but the Spanish style was reminiscent of the pomp of former ages. On the beach the young girls offered themselves without shame, even if you were with your partner. In the hotel our Cuban guide, during lunch, wrapped the leftover meat and other food that we hadn't finished in paper napkins and put this away in a sack tied to his belt. Responding to our looks of curiosity he explained, without embarrassment, that he would take the food home where they usually saw meat just a couple of times a month.

I had just started to play golf and it was automatic for me to ask if there was a course close to the hotel. One afternoon while the others were resting, the guide, took me to what was, at the time, the most beautiful course in Cuba. It was the course where thousands of American tourists had played at the time of Batista. There was a covering of dry grass after the summer drought and you could recognize the greens only by their position surrounded by bunkers. In one corner, close to what should have been a fabulous clubhouse, there were a couple of rusty clubs with the metal shaft re-covered with a coating of imitation bamboo. A truly desolate place. The guide took me to a bar close by where I could see photos showing Che Guevara playing golf in his combat uniform and military boots. The old barman still remembered the times of Batista and he showed me some photos of famous stars of the American cinema on the golf course, saying that in Varadero, the most touristic area on the island, they were re-constructing a golf course.

Today, with a view to promoting tourism on the island, in addition to revamping some existing old golf courses, they are constructing new courses to attract golfers from all over the world.

GRENADA

It was 1979. After five years teaching acupuncture in the USA together with Frank Warren and doctor Vorley of Detroit, we founded the "American Association of Acupuncture and Electrotherapy (AAAE)", of which many Americans and Canadians who had attended my courses, in the USA and Italy, became members. Doctor Vorley, owner, and fanatic, of a FIAT 124 Spider, always asked me to bring spare parts from Italy on each of my journeys to the US, parts that could not be found in the US. Following the foundation of the AAAE, the first international congress of the Association was organized, in collaboration with my Italian Association SIRAA (Società Italiana Riflessoterapia Agopuntura). The location chosen was that of the Caribbean island of Grenada with its subtropical climate and famous beaches, spices and also rather favorable prices. A month before the congress, a coup brought Maurice Bishop to power after years of dictatorship. He was a native of the island, graduated in law in the US, who installed a Marxist-Leninist regime allied to Fidel Castro. We were all a little concerned, but Vorley, through the doctors on the island, our students and friends of the new President, not only contacted Bishop, but they also convinced him to participate in and sponsor a dinner in our honor. Invitations to the dinner were widely sought by many interested parties, desiring to be introduced to the international scene, above all from the Americans.

Following a particularly adventurous flight, in a small plane that stopped at almost all the Caribbean islands I arrived in Grenada with about forty Italian students where we were greeted with great enthusiasm by the local authorities. We were the first group of tourists to arrive on the island following the coup.

On the same day, a group of American participants arrived and I went to greet them at the airport. Many of them had brought their golf bags and were rather disappointed when they heard that there wasn't a course on the island. It was inconceivable for them that on an island in the Caribbean, a paradise, there would not be a golf course. With no fear in the following days, on the large beach in front of the hotel we improvised a small golf course like the one I'd seen many years before in Mauritiana. In the group of American doctor golfers there was Margaret, a female doctor who watched the game and who I got involved with in a special way.

One evening, after dinner, we took a relaxing walk in the dark, on the beach where during the day we had played golf. The sand was still warm from the tropical sun. Margaret and I lay there warming ourselves.

We were invited by the President to a gala lunch where doctor Vorley thanked Maurice Bishop for his hospitality and asked him to consider constructing a golf course, for the benefit of tourism. A suggestion that he accepted very positively. For the occasion, as I only had casual clothing, Leonello, a dear student who always traveled with an impressive wardrobe, lent me a blue suit. Leonello was as tall as me but a lot slimmer. I kept the jacket open but had problems buttoning the trousers. On arriving at the gala dinner I was immediately sorry that I'd borrowed the suit, looking at the American doctors, excluding doctor Vorley, almost all were without a jacket and some were even wearing bermuda shirts.

As President of the Congress I was at the table with Maurice Bishop and his wife and after dinner she asked me to dance a salsa meringue. As soon as we launched ourselves into the dance I heard a strange sound. The pants had torn all along the seat. Fortunately, the jacket was quite long and partly covered the strange opening, but after that dance I didn't get up from my seat again.

The return journey was quite extraordinary. We left on the usual small plane that had brought us to the island, we arrived in Barbados, where we should have taken a Caribbean Airline flight to New York from where we would fly with Lufthansa to Italy. In Barbados we were informed the Caribbean airline had declared bankruptcy. It was high tourist season, all other airlines were fully booked and there were no seats available for our group. Only after two days, spent in an enforced vacation on the beach and visiting various golf courses, did we manage to find seats with Lufthansa for Bolivia, and from there to Atlanta, Toronto, London and finally, after a journey of over 36 hours we arrived in Turin.

A few years later, President Bishop, was toppled and shot in a coup backed by the USA, who, after bloody battles, occupied the island.

Today in Grenada there is a small 9 hole golf course that will be enlarged to 18 holes – but I don't know if it was Bishop that had it constructed.

THE CARNIVAL (the largest cruise ship in the world)

One morning checking my e-mail at the golf club I open a mail from SMS Cruises. It had been sent to all the golf clubs in Italy to present the new cruise ship that would be in service a few months later and was at that time the largest cruise ship in the world. On board a Golf Academy was planned, a golf school with various simulators and artificial putting greens. Those replying to a question-naire on golf, would be entered in a lottery to win an invitation for the inaugural voyage of three days .

As an old sailor I wasn't particularly interested in a cruise on the Atlantic but my experience, at the age of twenty, of a few months wor-king as a ship boy on an old cargo vessel provoked me to respond. I won the prize and at the beginning of June I spent three days with my partner on this colossal ship which had ten restaurants, uncountable bars and almost three thousand passengers.

On the highest deck there was the golf simulator where an American professional tried to convince passengers to take part in a course by making spectacular demonstrations hitting numerous balls, not only in the simulator, but also out to sea. This scene reminded me of the cruise I'd taken in the Caribbean islands many years before, on the ship of a New York estate agent and a few months before in Florida with my friend Marzio, when we had caught a small shark. When we gutted the shark to clean it and cook on the grill (fantastic dish) we found a golf ball in its stomach.

It is the habit among Americans and golf tourists, on cruises in the Gulf of Mexico, to compete to see who can hit the longest ball out to the sea. Who knows how many of these balls are swallowed by fish?

There followed three disappointing days. The first day I spent ins-pecting every corner of the ship to understand all its details, from the perfectly organized operating theatre, to the spa where men and wo-men spent all their time undergoing every type of beauty treatment for their skin and other areas. The other two days, not being the type to sunbath, like most of the other passengers, after dining in half the restaurants and having tried out various super packed night time bars and after hours spent in a splendid luxury cabin with my partner, I couldn't wait to return to dry land.

MYRTLE BEACH

Something that always struck me on American golf courses is the almost complete absence of women, above all in the southern states. I often asked the reason for this, especially in Georgia and Alabama, and American friends have always responded that just as was traditional in old England, golf was a sport exclusively for men. Myrtle Beach, in South Carolina, is one of the many golf paradises in America. There are more than sixty 18 hole courses, designed by the most famous architects and professionals. It was well worth it to have driven additional hours the previous day from SunnySide, to reach this immense Resort suggested to me by my friend John Gill. I was shocked to play at South Creek Golf Course, one of the most beautiful courses in the area, designed by the famous Arnold Palmer, costing 35 dollars (22 euro) including car. On this occasion as I was alone and hadn't booked a tee off time, I was invited by the master to wait for another lone player. When a player arrived it turned out to be a young lady, rather attractive, who was very happy to accept the invitation to play an Italian. She was called Carol and played very well, but after the introductions she concentrated on the game. She covered much of the ground on foot, leaving me driving the car, it was as if she was avoiding making conversation with someone she'd just met and was deep in thought, refusing all my attempts at conversation. The course was really as it had been described, a luxury course with perfect fairways and greens, well set out with water hazards and treacherous bunkers in a beautiful natural environment already revealing the colors of Autumn. Arriving at the ninth hole, we stopped a moment at the clubhouse to have a drink and I discovered the tragic comedy that I will now explain to you. After two hours playing she seemed to be more relaxed and more sociable and while we were drinking I asked if she lived in this area. She responded that at this moment she was on an enforced vacation, following a rather stressful and depressing divorce. She told me that she was staying in a hotel on the sea and she would be staying for a few more days. I began to fantasize, already thinking of inviting her to dinner to help her get over her depression or at least enjoy herself a little. I could already picture her in my arms trying to forget the recent past, when I had the terrible idea of asking what type of work she did. She was an anaesthesiologist, she told me smiling. I'm a surgeon I replied, smiling back. I should never have told her, she became very pale and almost hysterical looking. " Oh no please" she said and disappeared to the changing rooms. I didn't understand what had happened, I looked around to see if some kind of monster had arrived in the clubhouse and waited for her to return. Many minutes passed and in the meantime I met other players who had been behind us. We missed or should I say lost our turn. When Carol reemerged from the bathroom she seemed to have regained her composure. "I'm sorry," she said, "I've spent my whole life with surgeons, the husband who I divorced was one of your colleagues, he destroyed me and ruined my life, you surgeons are all bastards, fuck you," and she left leaving me standing at the bar. I was left speechless, I didn't know what to do, what to say. My dreams, my plan for the evening vanished in a moment. I was alone. I didn't even get to finish the course.

CALLAWAY GARDEN

C allaway isn't just the name of a famous golf equipment maker, it is also a common surname in the USA. The man in question was the rich owner of 14,000 acres of land who, one day, tired of property that didn't provide him any return and decided to fulfil his dream: an immense vacation complex in an unpolluted environment the likes of which only exists in Georgia, in the Pine Mountains region. In the USA they are called "Mountains" the height that we, in Europe, consider hills.

In the middle of these 'mountains' Callaway Gardens was born. A golf resort famous in all the southern states, with three championship courses, one of which was closed, waiting to weather the financial crisis of 2009. All around there were immense forests, inhabited by gigantic deer, raccoons, foxes, wild boar and other subtropical wild animals. When I was there for the first time in 1990, they told me that a few years before they had caught the last surviving puma in the park.

Almost hidden in the middle of the forest are cottages, perfectly equipped for guests in search of peace. Just outside the complex there is a large hotel for congresses and small conferences. In one corner of the park there's a 'Butterfly House', with thousands of butterflies from all over the world. In the middle of the Resort there's a huge lake where, in summer, water ski competitions take place and on the shore a long beach created using sand transported from nearby Florida.

The fairways of the golf course are very broad and forgive many errors, slices or hooks. The course is the darling of players arriving from every corner of Georgia, nearby states and abroad. The course is spectacular with a perfect mantle of grass and smooth greens like billiard tables. It is used by a multitude of players dressed in the most extravagant way. It's here that I got to see a player dressed in true wild west style with a huge cowboy hat, boots with overshoes, like galoshes, with studs in the sole. In the extremely well equipped pro shop you could find magnificent golf sandals (open and with studs), like those horrible but very comfortable ones worn by the Germans who arrive in Italy for the summer. In addition, I saw women wearing, without inhibition, outfits that on our courses would horrify our female players, scandalized by the exposed back and thighs, but above all because the majority of the wearers really didn't suit such clothes.

At the entrance to the Resort the guard directs you towards the building you need. There's a private golf club for members or those very few privileged guests who can afford the green fee of around 100 dollars, depending on the season. For the other two courses (when open) the tariff ranges from 40 to 60 dollars depending, not only, on the season but also on the fact that the two courses have different characteristics and therefore different prices. Obviously, the price of the car is always included in the green fee.

Recently, on this course I played followed by a group of Chinese people gesticulating and yelling at every well hit shot, so much so that the 'master' had to intervene and request calm and that they not yell like coyotes. This reminded me of a Chinese player who was a guest at la Girasoli. I was in the administrative office of the club, directly next to the car park so was able to help with his arrival. A presidential Mercedes 500 driven by a bodyguard pulled up, the Chinese driver/body guard opened the rear door while a second body guard opened the boot to take out a huge golf bag and suitcase. From the back seat emerged a very special character: no taller than a meter and a half, with jacket and tie and thick glasses. In the office, he introduced himself in perfect English while a bodyguard, without once opening his mouth, took out his wallet and paid the green fee. I introduced myself and he explained that he was in Turin for business without going into details. He had chosen our course following the advice of a friend who'd described it as the only 18 hole organic golf course. He re-emerged from the changing room in the same jacket and tie but now with sports trousers and golf shoes. I acted as his guide until the first tee, very curious to see how he played. The contrast between this person and the two bodyguards was astonishing; the latter were at least 1metre 90 tall and weighed over a hundred kilos with the typical face of a 'bad guy' in action films. After a couple of warm up swings the first drive; carried out almost to perfection, sending the ball almost 200 meters down the middle of the fairway. The small Chinese gentleman gave me a wave and continued on the course followed by his two companions. A few hours later a number of members explained to me how the balls that finished in the rough were collected by two Chinese giants while the player looked around waiting for their return, smoking one cigarette after another.

At the end of the round returning to the clubhouse they stopped at the restaurant where, besides ordering a vintage Barolo, the most expensive wine, the small Chinese man insisted on treating us to a bottle of Champagne to " drink with my staff" complementing me on the "natural" nature of the course, that he had appreciated immensely.

MAROCCO

More than 15 years have passed since I took a vacation in Morocco. As well as a winter break and to get to know a country as yet unknown to me I was also keen to play a couple of the courses that I'd heard about from various golf instructors. I was also interested in organizing golf trips for some of my members. The golf instructors can be found in Marrakech, or Agadir, where with their students they hold 'golf clinics' during the cold winter months when at home the snow and the cold prevent or at least dissuade golfers for playing. The piazza and the souk in Marrakech where two extraordinary discoveries for me. I'd passed many months in various African countries and was struck by the extreme variety of goods from every corner of the African Continent, but above all I was surprised by the cleanliness of the markets which compared with others in nearby countries had almost the orderliness of those in Switzerland. The Palmeraie Hotel had been chosen for my stay. I was informed that a new 18 hole course of particular interest had just been completed. I was pleasantly surprised, when introducing myself as the chairman of my club to the director of the club, that the former immediately offered us free entry to play. It was the second time that this had happened in a Club outside Italy, the first was in Kenia. I returned the favor a few evenings later by inviting him and his wife to dinner at one of the best restaurants in the city and I made him promise to be my guest at my club if he should every visit Italy (something that never happened).

The Golf Club of Palmeraie was built next to a hotel in the middle of the sand dunes of the desert little more than a year before and left a lot to be desired as far as a grassy mantle. The course was a bit flat, given some form by small artificial hills and adorned with young plants that were still supported to prevent the desert winds from taking them away. The caddies were formidable, I remember one in particular, Houssam, who, like the caddie in Nairobi supplied me with the direction and the correct line to reach the greens, a real instructor who after the first few holes had me make a score that almost ranked in the first category (I was actually in the third).

The course at Agadir where I found myself two days later, was practically managed by Club Med and overflowing with instructors and students from all over Europe, such that you had to join a long queue before being able to start a round and then we were rudely interrupted by a strong thunderstorm. I found myself in the packed Club House next to an Italian who spoke of the area like a regular visitor, until I realized that for a few years now, having reached pensionable age, he had decided to remain in Morocco where he'd started to play golf. He had been an Enel employee (the largest electricity supplier in Italy). During a vacation in Morocco, to celebrate his retirement with his wife he discovered that with his retirement funds he could purchase a villa by the sea, which in Italy would have been prohibitively expensive and, with his pension, could afford to employ a couple of people and live without difficulty, at the same time saving a decent amount. On returning to Italy, he met with his family; children and grandchildren and just a few weeks later he and his wife were established in Agadir. He never thought to take up golf initially and passed his time fishing in the sea at the front of his home. After a short time he began to get bored and felt homesick for Italy, so much so that he thought of returning. A meeting in the bar with an Italian golfer decided his future. The enthusiasm of the golfer was contagious and he was tempted to try and take a couple of lessons on the "Dunes". The game was up, the golf virus had infected him and his destiny lay before him. The boredom passed just like his nostalgia for Italy and he stayed in Morocco where he's been for many years.

Returning to Marrakech this time it was the turn of the Royal Golf Club. We'd booked the tee times a few days before, but when we arrived punctually at our assigned time we found ourselves in a queue behind important guests of the Moroccan government and had to wait. The Director of the club made his profound apologies and offered us a drink as consolation and to offset the heat of the early afternoon. But after we had played the first five holes of this beautiful course we were intercepted by the same director, this time even more embarrassed, explaining that we must leave the course for reasons of security as the king was about to arrive. We were so annoyed that the director, to excuse himself (for something that wasn't his fault), as well as refunding us our green fees also offered us two free green fees for the following days. Shame that the next day we were leaving for Italy. Somewhere I still have those vouchers. Who knows if after fifteen years they are still valid?

THE PASTURES WITH MR. GULL

M r Bob Gull is a constructor I met in at the home of friends in Atlanta. He lived in Columbus and when I told him that I was a few miles from his city we arranged to meet for dinner. A few days later he invited me to his Club, a private, very exclusive and very elegant club where huge Georgian style villas, owned by members, had been constructed along the fairways. The driving range was beautiful: five to six greens on the flat or on small hills, at various distances at which to address your shot and see the ball, if well played, land next to the flag. The balls were free and all game balls, not the usual practice balls, light and less effective. The cars were almost all luxury Club cars, with large fridges for drinks and GPS. The course was perfect with undulating, pristine fairways containing numerous water obstacles and bunkers in abundance completed with large 500 square meter greens that allowed putts from 30 meters. Bob, like his friends with whom he played, was an excellent player and said he was 10 HCP. After the first 9 holes we stopped for a snack at an abundant buffet, while nearby on an enormous stone positioned on a grill huge steaks were being cooked for those who'd finished playing and were treating themselves to a good meal washed down with a choice from the two Michelin star wine cellar.

Surveying the medal cabinet of the Club, with the names of the winners and the various course records, I asked Bob how many competitions he participated in each year. To my surprise he replied that he hadn't participated in any competitions for years now other than that of his friend the Chairman to which he was invited every year. When I asked how his HCP was determined he simply replied, "the average of my results on the course and my golfing companions".

This description could apply to many luxury American courses but it the more interesting when compared to the next time that Bob called to invite me to a game with some of his friends.

The first thing that surprised me was that the appointment was for the next day in the middle of the afternoon. He called to collect me at about four telling me that we'd meet our golf companions at the home of a friend. I found myself a short time later in front one of those enormous American houses, style "Gone with the Wind" and some time after with a glass in my hand surrounded by wealthy Georgian entrepreneurs and professionals asking what on the earth I was doing in Georgia, a state certainly not famous as a tourist spot.

They asked where I had played, when the owner of the house invited us to take our irons and Bob told me to take a wood, and some irons, without including the putter. A few minutes later we found ourselves, with about ten golfers, behind the huge house, at the beginning of meadows and forests extending for over 4000 acres. In a radius of 500 meters around us, as well as numerous heads of cattle quietly grazing, standing out, blowing in the wind I could see, six flags of different colors. As the only foreign guest I was invited to hit the first ball towards the green flag (the color denoted a par three). In just over an hour we'd played the six holes. When you arrived a putts distance from a flag, the "hole", that wasn't there, was given. Bob told me that they often played in the meadows, giving the sense that they had gone back in time, when golf was at its dawn. Here, as well, there was a rule about collecting and placing a ball when it had been hit into a cowpat, to avoid undesirable spraying. The group was followed by trailer loaded with drinks and beer and the evening concluded with a barbeque of generous steaks.

I had a really good time and the experience reminded me of other meadow-courses I'd played in Austria and Iceland. I also remembered the elegant Country Golf Club where Bob had hosted me just a few days before and the title of this book comes to mind **"from the stars to the stalls"**.

LUXOR

O nly when visiting Egypt can you really understand the meaning of the adjective "pharaonic" used to describe important human works. I had to been to Cairo in the past for some medical congresses, but I had actually never really been outside the hotels, hosting the congress, or at least only for an evening trip in the city. Only recently have I dedicated a whole week to explore and understand the various monuments of the Pharaones, a trip that concluded with a visit at the Golf Club in Luxor.

It was late afternoon, when the temperature wasn't as suffocating, when I arrived, having overpassed the area of the airport. The club house and office, to be great disappointment, were closed and the only thing I could do was make a quick tour of the course. The course was actually a copy of that of the Palmeraie Golf Club or the Alkemis in Marrakech in Morocco where I'd played years before. Surrounded by desert and the same type of hills, the same palms, the small grassy coat, the greens were a bit patchy but well trimmed.

Noticing two players ahead, the only ones on the course, dressed in a strange way that I couldn't recognize, as I got closer I realized that they were wearing the traditional Egyptian Galabia that reached to the ground. I was shocked to see this strange costume but I realized immediately the reason when the two players joined us. They were two maintenance workers who, as the course was closed, were having fun playing. They both lived just outside the Club and also played the role of the guards to the building. While we were chatting we were interrupted by the roar of a jet landing at the nearby airport, passing no more than fifty meters above our heads, we couldn't hear ourselves think, this reminded me of my many experiences at the course in Abidjan on the Ivory Coast. When I commented on this disturbance the two guards told me that as there were so few planes landing at the airport of Luxor that is really wasn't a problem. Only during military maneuvers, at the military airport next to the civilian one, when there was a continual movement of jets did the noise not, only interrupted play, but also caused the windows of the clubhouse to shake. My advice for anyone interested in playing this course is to check first if there are any military maneuvers planned or a higher than usual number of charter flights due to land at the airport.

BIOT

O n the Cote d'Azur there are some splendid golf courses, for every kind of player and for every purse, but the course at Biot has something special. It was also one of the first courses built in the area. It was actually first constructed in 1930 and endured several events, was abandoned for a few years and recently reemerged with a new owner. It's a short and relatively easy 18 hole, completely on the flat, with parallel holes and surrounded by houses.

On my arrival I met the golf pro and we had a chat. He had little to do and elaborated on various themes.

After I'd finished playing, completing the course in less than three hours, I returned to the Pros hop and made some comments regarding the course, that is particularly short and easy. When the Pro realized that I was chairman of a club in a resort with three courses he began to talk more candidly, beginning with the comment, "this is a course for pensioners," and continuing, "almost all the residents of the near-by houses are old and would not manage to play on a difficult course and this, for them, is the ideal course. It isn't tiring, there aren't any obstacles and you're finished in a few hours". I was with a beginner golfer friend who had finally managed to make his first par. He was really pleased with himself and I'm sure that he will always remember Biot as a fantastic golf course. Each to their own.

RHODES (what a disappointment)

The Afandou Golf Club in Rhodes was a real let down. Owned by the government it was built in the 1970's at the request of the then Greek President, a golf fan, in order to promote tourism. For a few years it had reasonable success attracting golfers from all over the world, but like almost all state owned institutions that are interesting for the minority, after a short time and various changes of government, it began to fall into decline due to lack of funds for tenance. The building works for the Club House were interrupted, and those of the guests quarters and other structures necessary for maintenance and today (2010) it looks like a building site that's been abandoned for years. A manager who was desperate about this situation explained the story of the course to me. It was built in a charming location, on the edge of the sea, in a Mediterranean forest full of every kind of plant, in a luxurious landscape and was a course with an interesting and creative design created by a famous architect. Despite its derelict state the green fee is rather expensive (30 euro). A prefabricated shack houses the office and bar. When I arrived I had to wait while the girl serving in the bar finished dealing with a customer before she could then take up her duties as the receptionist. I started to play with a friend and we met an American who now lived in Rhodes. He had become a member of the club at a cost of 300 euro (it certainly isn't worth more) and played almost every day. He said that the membership comprised about 20-30 foreigners which didn't suffice to maintain the course in a decent state. The fairways are covered with marine sand carried by the wind with rare areas of grass and at the sides there are many spiny and unkempt bushes. The previous evening there had been a heavy shower and there were many stagnating puddles. On one hole running alongside the road there were mountains of rubbish dumped or thrown from cars. Despite everything, it was a beautiful day, with the perfume of the sea air and wild flowers and we enjoyed ourselves, especially me used to play on the sand of the Sahara desert and in Icelandic and Georgian pastures. Halfway round the course we meet the only green keeper that the Club can afford to employee. With a helical grass trimmer he is cutting the grass of the green by hand, or rather, the grasses on the green, grass of every kind. He only speaks Greek and I don't manage to communicate well with him. He confirms, however, that for the maintenance of all 18 holes there is only himself, and with gestures, that many years ago the course was undoubtedly in much better condition, with three employees tending to the greenery. Now he has to do everything himself, working only part-time as they can't afford to pay him full time, but he is so attached to the place that he also comes to work unpaid overtime.

Contented with the walk in a beautiful Mediterranean pine forest, playing primordial golf, I meet the manager who'd explained the story of the decline of the course to me. He knows some of the FIG (Italian Golf Federation) managers and asked me to send his regards to those he knows personally. He wants to refund the green fee which I obviously refuse to accept, thinking about the poor solitary green keeper.

I happily accept a cold beer as he tells me that the state is negotiating with a foreign company that should complete the course, complete the various buildings and give back lustre to what was, 30 years ago, the most beautiful course in Greece. Let's hope so.

FORT BENNING

I t's the largest military base in the USA since the American government decided to close almost all the other small bases spread around the country to defend the land from a possible foreign invasion. It has become a large metropolis teeming with military and civilian assigned to the services based in the periphery of Columbus, the second largest city in Georgia.

Playing one day, at the Red Oak Country Golf Club in Cassetta, together with a local vice sheriff, who invited me to play with him some days later at Fort Benning. At the entrance there's a checkpoint where all visitors are inspected. After a few kilometers there's the golf course of the base, three nine hole courses given the names of three distinguished generals. After registering at the office we go on to the first tee. After two practice swings I'm about to make my first shot when my movements are rudely interrupted by a burst of machine gun fire disturbing my concentration leaving me with one arm in mid air. The sheriff smiles and informs me that it will be like this for almost the whole course. The course is a few hundred meters from the light artillery practice range, but I must admit that after a couple of holes we hardly noticed the thundering of the weapons. Though a couple of times we jumped from the roar of some gun, bazooko or armed tank shooting in the distance, all inside a base the size of an Italian region . The course is very well kept, built in the middle of forests of Georgian pine and oaks, naturally animated and full of deer continually crossing the fairways, especially in the evenings. The animals are inquisitive of both the players and the crackle of artillery. The greens are very small, some even smaller than those of the Girasoli, often perched on small hills and if you go a little long, your ball will inevitably fall over the other side leaving you have to make another approach.

Halfway round the course we are in the middle of the fairway, having hit our balls, when we hear a whistle. We turn around to see two youths shaved to "zero", marine cut, who ask to pass. The sheriff makes the sign to go ahead and we move over into the rough. Two nice shots pass us and I see two soldiers, with two small bags on their backs containing a few irons, running towards us. They salute us as they pass to reach their balls. The sheriff explains to me that the youths are probably part of the golf team on the base and that they are training for a rather special golf championship: teams of 2 or 4 players in a race against time to complete the course, naturally the score also counts! The time taken for 18 holes is reduced to 90-100 minutes. A killer.

Nice and easy with our golf car we complete the round and we stop for a beer at the office before returning home. I'm struck by a vision in the car park : an old Fiat 600, 1960s, parked in the corner with the license plate of Georgia and next to it the old Italian license plate of Naples. The manager of the golf club explained that car belonged to an old retired general who lived on the base. When he was a captain he had served in Naples and when repatriated he brought along the old car he'd bought in Italy.

I had a great time that day and I've returned many times to play taking with me many Italian friends, but I've never seen that old 600 again.

IS ARENAS

O n the west coast of Sardinia, following years of battle with a fanatical environmentalist, who had delayed the development work, one of the most beautiful golf courses in Italy was realized. It's always a delight to play here whenever I find myself in Sardinia. The course is immersed in a pine forest, built to protect the internal land from the invasion of sand delivered by the Maestral, it's a course reminiscent of some Californian courses beaten by the wind for many days of the year. Is Arenas is the name of the white beach skirting the course and from which it is separated by hills of sand. I witnessed the birth of this course and I'd played the first 3 holes. Pier Maria Pellò was the craftsman who fought for years to complete the course. I still recall his telephone calls to compare notes at the beginning of construction. Immediately afterwards, however, the work was halted due to the intervention of environmentalists. They declared that nature shouldn't be touched and should be left as it is. If they really wanted things this way, they would have had destroy the pine forest returning the area to its original form, a long stretch of uncultivated sand, with the classic, short Mediterranean bushes bent by the wind, with the sand invading the land and closing the local roads. In an area where fires are the order of the day, golf course provide real barriers to block the spread of fire, barriers that are often created in other such areas just for this purpose. It's the usual class war between those who consider golf a sport reserved only for the rich and therefore condemnable, And results from ignorance about the spread and popularity throughout the world of this sport, where it is practiced by all social classes, from the laborer to the miner, from the employee to the entrepreneur. It was the situation, until a few years ago in Italy, where courses were built copying the most beautiful in the world, those reserved for VIPs, with enormous investments, exaggerated management costs and therefore restricted to those who could afford it, those vulgarly called "rich and stupid". The situation has changed dramatically in the last few years and today anyone can start to play this sport just as they are free to take up skiing or tennis, as there are now courses that have been constructed on a budget with low management costs. Today in many clubs it costs less to play golf than to fund a ski season but the general sentiment remains that golf is an elite sport.

CASTELGANDOLFO

This name, for most people, is associated with the summer residence of the catholic pope in the Alban hills, an area of volcanic origin, with many lakes and a temperate climate. For centuries the location of the summer villas of the rich roman aristocrats. With the decline of the roman empire the area was almost abandoned and in the 6th century was acquired by a noble family from Genoa "the Gandolfi", a name commonly heard in Liguria and Piedmont. Consider that my grandmother was also called "Gandolfi", but she was anything but noble.

The Gandolfi built the famous castle that still carries their name and that was bought at the end of the 1500 by the Vatican.

A few hundred meters from the papal residence there was a crater, already dormant for centuries, whose base, full of water, had become an forest with centuries old Mediterranean pines and citrus groves. On the edge of the crater, a Cardinal, nephew of a pope, had a splendid villa built to host his lover with the exotic name of : "Pavona". Still today the villa from the 60s that now serves as the clubhouse of the Golf course has the same name: " La Pavona" that is also the name of the surrounding area.

The 18th hole designed by Trent Jones, respecting the local cultivation, unfurls between small lakes and knolls which make the course very technical and demanding. The starting point at the edge of the crater is beautiful from the tee of the first hole to that of the twelfth, from where you can follow the trajectory of the ball which flies and falls in the middle of the fairway at the base of the crater.

Every time I visit Rome I always try to play this course and if you go you might find yourself playing alongside those so famous politician, stars of the screen or international jet set, some cardinal or other and many, many Americans, all golfers obviously.

I have never met the pope there, but as far as I'm aware there haven't been too many golf playing popes.

CYPRUS

When I did my military service in the 60s, I was sent for a few weeks to Cyprus in a military hospital, during the clashes between the Turkish and Greek population. As I didn't play I wasn't particularly interested in golf and the bullets flying between one side and the other prevented us from moving freely so we couldn't leave the military camp. I returned to Cyprus more than 40 years later. It was another world. This time I went in search of the famous courses that allow you to play all year round, in a particularly favorable climate.

It was the month of March and I was rather unlucky because for the whole three days the whole island suffered a kind of tropical rain: impossible to play. I promised myself however that I would in any case visit the three courses mentioned by all travel agents and I visited all three. The oldest course, built in 1994, is the Minthis Golf Club, a course in the middle of the mountains with a residential village of dubious taste, not really in harmony with the local architecture. It could have been the rain or because it was the end of winter but all the courses were incredibly green. One of my companions told me that during summer some of the courses leave something to be desired. The Aphrodite Golf Club is without a doubt the one that I liked the most together with the Secret Valley. The third day they told me about a golf course considered family friendly and managed by the owner. They told me that the most interesting aspect of the club was the home style cooking, the best in all the clubs on the island. It was true, the food was excellent, I couldn't compare it, however, with those courses where I hadn't dined. The family owners were incredibly nice. Immediately after lunch, during a very brief break from the rain, they had me play a round of 9 holes: a very rustic course, green in winter and completely dry in summer with frequent areas of earth. There was no irrigation system. During the hot months players carried a small carpet of synthetic grass around with them on which to place the ball. This reminded me of my experience in the Sahel desert in Mauritania. It really is true; where there is the passion for golf you manage to play absolutely anywhere.

SHANGHAI INTERNATIONAL GOLF
AND COUNTRY CLUB

During the 70s, from 1971 onwards, when I found myself in China (The People's Republic of China) to study acupuncture, golf wasn't in my thoughts. When I visited again in 1998 one of the first things that I asked of old Mr Lee, owner of the site where they built boats, that they imported in Italy, was the existence of a golf course at the time of the foreign delegation at the beginning of the 1900. He didn't know anything but promised to find out and let me know.

When I returned two months later not only did he tell me that, a few days earlier, the first golf course in Shanghai had been inaugurated but he explained that, from an old friend, he knew that the English, in collaboration with the Americans, at the beginning of the 1900 had built a 9 hole course, on the bank of the yellow river (Hiang Tze Kiang) where various diplomats and commercial delegations played. After it had been abandoned by the foreign delegation the course quickly disappeared engulfed by the fluvial vegetation. I was very interested in the new course and called to arrange a visit introducing myself as Chairman of my own Club. I was met on arrival by the manager who as well as having me sign the guest book (I was the first visitor who was Chairman of a foreign Club) immediately offered me a day pass reserved for special guests and they accompanied me on a visit of the course and its buildings. The clubhouse was an enormous building with two distinct structures that, in my opinion, had little to do with Communist China. One was elegant and sober for the public and one reserved for VIP guests where in the bathrooms the solid gold taps gleamed, at least that's what the manager told me. To this day I don't know if my companion's words were true or not. On the course tens of workers were still putting in order hundreds of decorative plants that framed perfect fairways and greens. The course was practically deserted of players and, when at the end of the tour I started to play, with a golf bag lent to me for the occasion, on a golf car driven by a tiny caddy who spoke almost perfect English. In little more that two hours I completed the round devoured by tens of bites delivered by ferocious mosquitoes.

Before playing, I'd practiced a little on the multi-story driving range, where an American professional had recently been engaged to give lessons to the first Chinese to try this sport.

I was sure that golf would develop very well in China where everyone is sport mad, especially for ball sports. During lunch with Mr Lee I asked what he thought of starting to build golf courses for the masses, at low cost, as I'd done in Italy with the Girasoli. I could have collaborated with him in such a project. He responded that he was really too old to start new activities but that he would think of someone that might be interested. There was no follow up and I have regretted it ever since, having seen how golf has developed in China in the interim years.

LEROS THE GOLF QUARRY

In the Dodecanese islands, the archipelago of Greek islands almost touching the Turkish coast. there is Leros, an island known as the island of the mad. Neglected by the tourist circuit for this reason but also due to the difficulties reaching the island and the lack of long beaches. This has also been the island's good fortune and has provided a defense against the attack of mass tourism that has destroyed many other islands.

"Island of the mad" because for some decades the island housed an "open" psychiatric hospital, where many families entrusted a number of psychiatric patients to be reinserted into normal life and into society. Previously Leros was home to the politically persecuted during the 'Regime of the Colonels'. In the end there were more than 4000 patients free on the island living a terrible existence, until a journalistic investigation revealed the mental decline of the patients and the decline of the island itself. The European Union forced the Greek government to close this concentration camp.

When I visited I fell in love. It was real love at first sight not just for me but many other foreign visitors among whom many Italians who have become residents. After various periods of vacation spent on the island I acquired a small olive grove where, other than old, ruined house, there was still the traces of an artillery station and ,spread among the bushes, there were pieces of Italian military vehicles from the times of the Italian occupation of the Dodecanese islands taken from the Turks, during the war of 1911. Leros was the most important Italian marine base for over 30 years and all over the island traces of Italy are still in evidence, from the architecture of the houses, public buildings, monuments and hospitals. For this reason the Italians have always been loved by the whole population of this island and were considered to be the liberators from the hated Turkish occupation that lasted over three centuries and the majority of the old islanders still speak the Italian learned at their school desks.

The only thing missing on this island, despite the fabulous sea and wind that powers my sailboat, is a golf course.

I've invited many Greek friends from Leros to Italy, to my club, entrusting them to one of my instructors I've started them off and infected them with the golf virus. They will join me in founding my next project; Leros Golf Club with its annexed 9 hole course. The project is in the promotion phase and I hope, that in just a few years, I'll manage to get it up and running, if all goes well and good health accompanies me.

This way I could spend longer periods on this splendid island. At the moment, after a couple of days I always miss my golf and feel the need to return home.

THE HONORARY MEMBERSHIP OF FIG
(Italian Golf Federation)

T his is the membership that the Chairman of the FIG (Italian Golf Federation) sends every year to all the Chairmen of golf clubs and various county representatives, regional Federations and, at the discretion of the Chairman, to all those who contribute or have contributed to the development of golf in Italy as well as many friends of friends, journalists, authorities.

The membership is very coveted because, as well as flattering those (at least some) who receive it, it provides free entrance to most Italian courses. When I became chairman of my club and received the membership I also experienced a certain satisfaction and a few days later, finding myself in Rome I immediately put my membership to work showing it at the Olgiata Golf Club. I was warmly welcomed by the manager who also offered me a drink and I played on the 18 hole course together with an advisor who explained the course to me. I few weeks later I found myself in a marine location where there was a 9 hole course where I encountered a small office with one employee playing the role of administrator, bar assistant, caddy master etc.

I didn't dare use my membership card, I paid the green fee and played very enjoyable seven, par three, and two, par 4, holes. To this day I use the membership, with all its advantages, exclusively at the golf clubs of my friends where, in fact, I don't even need to show it.

I've tried a couple of times to use the card abroad, but apart from one German club, even though I was always treated politely, I've always been asked to pay the green fee.

GOLF DIGEST- THE DISEASES

About twenty years ago the first articles began to appear in many medical publications regarding the toxic and carcinogenic effects caused by herbicides. Years before these articles, Chinese medical publications had already been published research into the devastating effects on the Vietnamese population caused by the defoliants used by the Americans during the Vietnam War. On one of my study trips to China at the beginning of the 70s I took the opportunity to spend some time in Hanoi to meet and see in action a doctor who used acupuncture in obstetrics. It was on this occasion, in a hospital, that I saw some patients suffering from incurable cutaneous lesions and various types of tumor. At the beginning of the 80s a dear agricultural worker friend of mine, died in just a few days from a acute hepatitis with liver necrosis, that the doctors attributed to products that he'd used to remove weeds from corn fields on his farm. The combination of these reports and personal experiences induced me to discontinue any cultivation, at my farm, that required the use of chemical products. Instead I dedicated my land to the cultivation of fodder for horses, transforming my farm into a riding centre and later its present role of golf complex. Some years later I had the opportunity to follow the construction of a golf course. The land was completely reworked, turned over and totally treated with herbicide, to destroy any kind of grass, even at the embryonic stage in order that later only the chosen type of grass could be sown and grown on the golf course. An engineer I knew managed this work and was present almost every day on the course. The work lasted a little more than one year. It was only just finished, and you could already play on the ncw 9 holes, when one day my engineer friend asked me for my diagnostic opinion, on a radiographic exam that he'd carried out a few days before as he'd been suffering digestive problems. The examinations revealed the presence of voluminous spots in the area of the liver. A tumor was diagnosed that, in just a few months, led to the death of the unfortunate engineer. In the years that followed I asked two of my instructors to make an informal enquiry into various courses where their friends taught. The results were really meaningful: in almost all the courses presenting the characteristics classical of the so-called "American courses" perfect fairways, smooth as billiard tables, characterized by the presence of just one type of grass, well protected from other grasses by the use of selective herbicides. Among the regular members (those who played almost every day), among some instructors and maintenance personnel, there were reported cases of tumors or hepatitis. As a result of such research, I consulted with the director of the Institute of Cancer Research (Istituto di Ricerca sul Cancro), who confirmed the increase of tumors in agricultural workers involved in rice production, where the same herbicides are used as those used on golf courses. I, therefore, wrote an article for the publication Golf World (Mondo del Golf) alerting everyone to the use of such products and listing the risks and effects. I was criticized by some for my initiative, that certainly didn't help the spread of golf but I was very pleased by the large number of emails that I received from golfers who were grateful to be warned of certain toxic effects of many chemical products used, not only on golf courses, but above all, and to a much larger degree, in agricultural production.

In June 2009 Golf Digest, the most prestigious American golf publication Golf published a long investigation on golf and its future. In one chapter of this article they dealt with pollution caused by golf courses with a very long list of all the pathologies discovered in many players and directly attributable to the frequency of time spent at the course and contact or inhalation of volatile residues of the substances used. I always remember a friend and dermatologist who told me that how he could recognize a golfer, from the characteristic cutaneous lesions that he found on patients. In the same article in Golf Digest they expressed the wish that golf would return to the old times, to the 30s, when no-one knew what a selective herbicide was and this sport was played on natural land, almost like at the dawn of time, where the only treated area was the green.

You can, therefore, understand that when I built the course at the Girasoli I decided to create it in the most natural way possible. In twenty years at this course we have never had a case of tumor apart from one player who had played at our club for just one year: he used to smoke four packets of cigarettes a day and was struck by lung cancer.

In the New York Times recently, there appeared, on the front page, an article on the inauguration of the first biological course in the USA also in the presence of President Obama, A course on which no chemicals will be used. Shame that the membership fee is 350,000 dollars and the annual subscription 12,000. These fees have absolutely nothing to do with "biological", on the contrary its discriminatory nature is highly polluting, creating a real "biological ghetto".

In any case I find it very strange because, according to my experience, a biological course from first construction to the final maintenance has, without a doubt lower costs than so-called VIP courses. And I ask myself where do they get the cheek to ask for those fees, but you know America is America.

14910562R00052

Made in the USA
Lexington, KY
10 November 2018